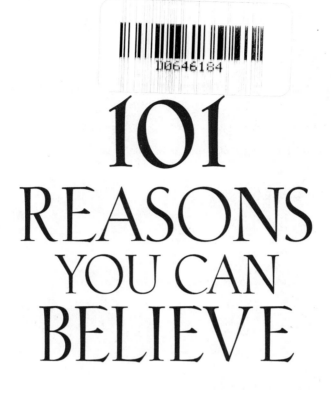

101
REASONS
YOU CAN
BELIEVE

Ralph O. Muncaster

HARVEST HOUSE PUBLISHERS

EUGENE, OREGON

Cover by Terry Dugan Design, Minneapolis, Minnesota

101 REASONS YOU CAN BELIEVE
Copyright © 2004 by Ralph O. Muncaster
Published by Harvest House Publishers
Eugene, Oregon 97402
www.harvesthousepublishers.com

Library of Congress Cataloging-in-Publication Data

Muncaster, Ralph O.
  101 reasons you can believe / Ralph O. Muncaster.
  p. cm.
Includes bibliographical references.
  ISBN 0-7369-1198-7 (pbk.)
  1. Apologetics. I. Title: One hundred one reasons you can believe. II. Title: One hundred and one reasons you can believe. III. Title.
  BT1103.M86 2004
  239—dc22   2003020636

Printed in the United States of America

04 05 06 07 08 09 10 11 12 /BP-KB/ 10 9 8 7 6 5 4 3 2 1

To the staff of Harvest House Publishers

*Your steadfast contribution to every phase of the development
of my work has been a continuous inspiration, of which
I feel but a small part. Every day I am thankful that our
Lord has placed us together in mutual service
to help others know Him.*

Acknowledgments

To Terry Glaspey, Director of Acquisition and Development at Harvest House Publishers, for his help in the genesis and development of the concept and ideas behind this book.

To Paul Gossard, Project Editor at Harvest House Publishers, for his tireless, creative, and unselfish help on many of the books that I've authored.

Contents

Building Real Belief and Faith

Without faith it is impossible to please God...

Some people read these words from Hebrews 11:6 and conclude that they please God by believing in Him without question. Yet this kind of faith is flimsy. It's not the kind of faith God calls us to have. This becomes evident as we continue reading:

...because anyone who comes to him must believe
that he exists...

God wants us to rationally believe in Him. He asks us to test any authority proclaiming divine inspiration, as we learn from 1 Thessalonians 5:21: "Test everything. Hold on to the good." He wants us to use our minds to intellectually reason that He exists and is who He proclaims. Furthermore, He wants us to take action, believing

...that he rewards those who earnestly seek him.

If we earnestly seek Him, He will reward us—and one way is with real, reasoned belief, which will grow into a strong and lasting faith. Webster's dictionary says it this way:

> *Faith is* confident belief *in the truth, value,*
> *or trustworthiness of a person, idea, or thing.*

The following pages are a journey in belief and faith—in God, and in the evidence He has provided in the Bible and in everything He has made. So sit back, relax, and bring an open mind and heart to 101 reasons you can believe.

The Rose

Emily sat down beside the brook and marveled at the harmony and serenity of her surroundings. Water bubbled and swirled around the rocks in a pattern whose beauty was far beyond that of any human art. Every shade of green appeared in the foliage of the banks of the stream and the fields beyond. Overhead the sun shone brightly, and the spring afternoon was scented with daffodils. Butterflies were everywhere. Bees buzzed.

She looked at her feet and a splash of red caught her eye. Nestled among some pure white daffodils was a rose. *How odd,* she thought. *A single rose in all these daffodils.* She reached down and picked it, fascinated by its color, its shape, its form. The vivid red petals framed the bright yellow pistils tucked at the core of the flower. Drops of water beaded on the leaves. How intricate and precise was the detail of the tiny parts of the inside of the rose. She wondered what everything was for. She wondered how the rose "worked." Relaxing and enjoying its beauty, she closed her eyes and slowly raised it to her face. Its incredible softness touched her lips. Its fragrance kissed her nose.

Who would create such a thing? she wondered. *Why? For what purpose? Could this be evidence of a loving Creator richly rewarding His creation with pleasure?*

The Impossibility of the Random Origin of Life

Science can now assume that the random origin of life is impossible. This is because

❖ the molecular components necessary for the development of a living cell could not conceivably have come together in the manner required to allow it to work

❖ there is no known mechanism to place life into non-life, even if the components could come together

Simply assembling the components to create the simplest kind of a cell would have about 1 chance in $10^{112,827}$ of randomly happening.[1] Any mathematician would agree that these odds are virtually zero. The reason for this improbability is that many things are necessary for the key components of DNA and protein chains to work properly. First, the *chirality* (molecular orientation) must be perfect for both. Second, only life-specific amino acids must be used. Third, the amino acids must be put in the proper place. Fourth, the correct material must be put in the right place for the DNA molecule. Fifth, the sequencing of genes must be correct for the DNA molecule to function. All of these requirements must be fulfilled.

Further complicating the problem of proper assembly of the components of the first cell of life is the fact that time is limited. Even taking the largest scientific estimate of the age of the universe—fifteen billion years (10^{17} seconds)—there is not nearly enough time for such an improbable event to happen.

Finally, even if everything miraculously came together, life would still need to be added to non-living matter. We have never seen this happen, nor do we know how to make it happen.

The only alternative to the random "evolution" of the first living cell is special creation by a supernatural Source.

The Empty Tomb

Early in the morning the women went to the tomb where Jesus' body had been laid. They were heavily laden with spices to prepare His body, and were concerned about how they would enter the tomb because a large rock covered the entrance. No doubt their hearts pounded and their minds raced with thoughts at this last chance to see their master.

What shock upon their arrival! The Roman guards had disappeared, the stone had been rolled away, and Jesus was nowhere to be found! Where did He go? Who had moved Him?

That the tomb of Jesus was empty is, perhaps, the most important event in all of history. It is the foundation of Christianity—by far the largest and most influential organized movement of all time. Jesus had prophesied at least three times that He would rise from the dead in three days. And the true test of something being from God is perfect prophecy. This unique ability of God alone to know the end from the beginning is identified by the prophet Isaiah:

> *I am God, and there is no other;*
> *I am God, and there is none like me.*
> *I make known the end from the beginning,*
> *from ancient times, what is still to come.*
> —ISAIAH 46:9-10

Of course it is the eyewitness accounts of the risen Christ that directly affirm Jesus' fulfilled prophecy of His own resurrection. This prophetic affirmation also fulfills His claim to be God.

However, the empty tomb itself, with absolutely no corpse to be found, also affirms the resurrection. Both the Roman and Jewish authorities had every reason to produce a corpse of Jesus. It would have ended the rapid spread of Christianity once and for all. And there was certainly ample reason for the Roman and Jewish authorities to want to end Christianity. It was disrupting their political and religious control of the region. Within weeks it had spread to thousands of people. So alarmed were the religious leaders, that the apostles and early Christians were jailed and persecuted. Every attempt would have been made to locate the corpse of Jesus. And with the strength of the Roman government and influence of the religious leaders, there would have been extensive resources to conduct a vast manhunt for the corpse.

During the first century in Jerusalem, which was under Roman control, it would have been extremely difficult to obtain and hide the body of Jesus. First, very strict security precautions were carried out by arguably the greatest military machine ever assembled—the Roman army.

> "Take a guard," Pilate [the Roman governor] answered. "Go, make the tomb as secure as you know how."
>
> —MATTHEW 27:65

The Roman guard, under strict orders to protect the corpse of Jesus, faced the threat of crucifixion if they failed in their job. Considering the threat of death, the odds of all 16 guards failing (16 was the number of guards typically assigned to such a political prisoner) are unimaginable. (More about this in reason 6.)

Second, the Jewish Sabbath, which prohibited work, would have made any action to steal the corpse from the tomb religiously unacceptable to the Jewish populace. Third, the city of Jerusalem was relatively small, making it difficult to take and conceal a body without detection.

Finally, the authorities would have used every method possible to determine the actual fate of Jesus and the location of His corpse. This would have included bribery and threats of torture. Certainly, if there was anyone with information regarding a corpse of Jesus, someone would have "cracked" and provided information.

The evidence is clear and self-evident. The tomb of Jesus was empty, and nobody could produce a corpse to stop the rapid spread of Christianity. The authorities would have tried. The resurrection, the spread of Christianity, and its later rejection by the Jews all happened exactly as prophesied.

The empty tomb played an indispensable role in the start of Christianity, specifically helping verify that Jesus is God.

Thought

How is it that human beings can think at all, rather than simply behave based on instinctive responses like animals do? Our basic thought process is like this:

1. *Input of information is received:* historical information or current stimuli.

2. *Information is related to something:* knowledge, experience, or emotion. Humans process information based on relating it to something else, often knowledge of something they have learned, or past experiences or emotions; even "gut feel" when nothing else exists.

3. *Information is organized* based on priorities, which may take several forms, such as chronological ordering, emotional response, degree of impact, relevance, interrelationship with other information, and so on.

4. *New thoughts are formulated* based on the organized information. Such thoughts can take several forms, such as action, creativity, abstract thinking, emotional thinking,

logical thinking, reordering of priorities, or new ordering of chronology.

There is no evidence of the animal world possessing any such ability. We are told that we (but not animals) are created in God's own image (Genesis 1:26-27). Why would God give us the ability to think? We are told that one of the essential ways God wants us to love Him is with our minds (Mark 12:30). Is it possible that God gave us the capacity to think in order to love Him as completely as possible? The fact that we can think at all is evidence of God.

ATP Motors

Within each cell of a human body there are hundreds of intricate *ATP motors* that produce energy for the cell. These tiny motors are 200,000 times smaller than a pinhead. They spin constantly at a rate of 100 revolutions per second, day and night. Moreover, they produce about three new ATP molecules—fuel for the body—every second. Since there are as many as 100 trillion cells in the human body, everyone's body contains hundreds of trillions of these phenomenal ATP motors.

Engineers and scientists can only observe and marvel at this incredible feat of engineering, which is critical for human existence on a second-by-second basis. Nothing that humans have ever created even comes close to these motors in performance, durability, and size! An entire branch of science is developing—called *nanotechnology*—with a primary focus on mimicking the amazing mechanical engineering of things less than a billionth of an inch in size.

All the evidence points to only one possibility for the original nanotechnology "engineer": God.

The Roman Guard Protecting the Body of Jesus

Historical evidence, even from many non-Christian sources, indicates that Jesus was a real person and was crucified. However, only Christians claim that He later rose from the dead. The most common alternative answer for others to the issue of the "empty tomb" (see reason 3) is that the disciples stole the body. This is highly unlikely when one considers the professional Roman guard used to protect the corpse.

The Roman guard would have consisted of 16 soldiers for an important political prisoner like Jesus. These guards were typically arranged four on each side of whomever they were to protect. At night, four guards would have been placed directly in front of the entrance to the tomb with the other 12 sleeping "face in" in a semicircle in front of the four that were at watch. Guards slept in shifts so that there would always be a minimum of four on watch at a time. Any guard that deserted his post or fell asleep would face crucifixion.[2]

Some suggest that the guard posted was actually a Jewish Temple guard instead of the more formidable Roman guard. Even a Temple guard, though, consisted of ten well-trained men. However, evidence overwhelmingly suggests a Roman guard for the following reasons:

1. The Greek word *koustodia* (guard) was used, which at the time referred to a Roman guard.

2. The Roman governor Pilate issued the order, implying that he was in ultimate command of the guard. (If only a Temple guard had been requested, why would the Pharisees have gone to Pilate to request help?)

3. When the guards approached the Jewish religious leaders after the resurrection, they were obviously concerned about the reaction of Pilate, not that of the leaders themselves. This is evident from the leaders stating, "If this report [the report of the guards sleeping] gets to the governor, we will satisfy him and keep you out of trouble" (Matthew 28:14). If it had been only a Temple guard, which was under the authority of the religious leaders, serious consequences would have been faced immediately. In this case, the religious leaders were sought out by the guards to try to avoid a sentence of execution issued by the Roman authorities.

It would be highly unlikely that a frightened band of untrained disciples would be able to either sneak past or overcome a highly trained Roman guard. Nor would they want to, especially under penalty of death. Consider that there would be no benefit to be gained by them from a dead Messiah—one who had claimed to be God and had openly promised to rise again from the dead.

Therefore, the protection of the corpse by a Roman guard leads to the conclusion that the body of Jesus was not stolen—and that He in fact rose from the dead, indicating that He was who He claimed to be: God.

It Exists

Life exists. Matter exists. The universe exists. It's undeniable. Anything that exists requires a cause for its existence. What is the best explanation for this cause? God.

Israel

Yakov clutched his copy of the Scriptures as he jumped off of the boat that had arrived at the port of Tel Aviv. After running down the dock to a patch of ground, he fell to his knees, sobbing and giving thanks to God for his safe trip and for that special day. It was May 14, 1948. Israel had just become a nation.

When he regained his composure, Yakov's thoughts focused on the enormous importance of the day. He recalled the prophecy from Isaiah that the Jewish people had been looking to for centuries:

> *In that day the Lord will reach out his hand a second time to reclaim the remnant that is left of his people from Assyria, from Lower Egypt, from Upper Egypt, from Cush, from Elam, from Babylonia, from Hamath and from the islands of the sea.*
>
> *He will raise a banner for the nations and gather the exiles of Israel; he will assemble the scattered people of Judah from the four quarters of the earth.*
> —ISAIAH 11:11-12

The day had come. The Jews had been exiled from Israel a second time in A.D. 70 when the Romans had decimated the land.

Ever since, against all odds, the Jews had been looking forward to a return. Now it was happening.

What are the odds of such a thing happening? First of all, never in the history of mankind has a people maintained its pure identity after separation of more than a few generations from its homeland. The reason is the inevitable intermingling of races. We don't hear of Russian Philistines or German Edomites, yet we commonly refer to the Jews of various nationalities. However, God had promised the Jews that their name would always be "great," implying that they would maintain their identity.

> *I will make you into a great nation and I will bless you; I will make your name great, and you will be a blessing.*
>
> —GENESIS 12:2

So the Jews beat the odds by maintaining an identity.

Second, and more significantly, they *did* return to their homeland and establish a "great" nation. This is even more amazing when one considers the odds against this. Virtually the entire Arab world was amassed in a united front opposing them—including a vast army that immediately fought them. But the Jews, facing overwhelming numbers of enemy troops, soundly defeated them. In June of 1967, another stage of the prophecy was made complete when the again vastly outnumbered Israelis defeated the Arabs to gain control of Jerusalem.

Thousands of years ahead of time, the Bible correctly identified the incredible second return of the Jews. What does this mean?

God is in control.

God inspired the Bible.

The Beaver

The beaver is an amazing engineer and architect.

Imagine a fast-running river in Canada in early spring. Even a well-qualified human engineer would face many complex issues of how to build a dam to stop the rapid flow of water and provide a balanced ecosystem for the area. Imagine if he had to do it using only the trees, grasses, and mud in the area—and had to use only his teeth and the rest of his body.

Yet the beaver somehow knows how to do just that. Trees are felled, and branches are placed together at the site using an engineer-type plan that involves pulling in strong beam-like "stringers" and carefully sizing and placing support-sized branches. Once the basic support structure of the dam is in place, beavers start adding a mix of grasses, rock, and mud in an amazing "woven" pattern—at precisely the right moments to gradually stop the rushing waters, which eventually creates an artificial lake. The incredible dams engineered by beavers can be enormous in size. The largest ever recorded—located in Three Forks, Montana—was over a half-mile long (2140 feet), 14 feet high, and 23 feet thick.[3] Consider that the lead design engineer on this mammoth project was probably less than ten years old.

Beaver lodges (homes) are built by the colony of beavers living in the pond area. Each lodge is constructed using the same technique of developing a strong base structure, adding supporting structural members, and then covering this with a mat of grasses and mud to seal and insulate the structure. Beavers' strong, clawed front "arms" are uniquely suited for the task of building a lodge. They often cradle mud in these arms, holding it against their chests as they walk up the lodge roof on their hind feet. The lodges are usually about ten feet in diameter and can be entered only via a hidden underwater entryway.

The ecosystem established by beaver dams is beautiful, balanced, and complete. Beaver ponds allow new grasses and vegetation to grow, providing a breeding ground for mosquitoes and other insects. These in turn provide food for fish, which provide food for animals like bears. The ponds also provide a watering source for a multitude of other mammals, like rabbits and deer; an entire community of life develops.

Beavers not only know how to make dams, but also how to maintain and use them for their special purpose. The dams themselves form the basic ecosystem necessary for beavers themselves. The dams protect beavers from predators that attack from the land. So important are these dams in maintaining their environment that they are constantly being monitored and repaired by the beavers in the colony. Beavers also cleverly operate the dam to maximize the advantages of the system. In the winter, after the pond has frozen, they open the dam long enough to allow the water level in the pond to drop which provides air space under the ice. In that manner they can live much of the winter underwater, where they can eat trees stored underwater and hide from predators. When the spring thaw arrives, the levels return to normal.

Often we don't understand the purpose behind why creatures do what they do. In other cases, like that of the beaver, we can marvel at abilities that so closely resemble those of humans. We can observe the purpose behind the beaver's hard work. Not only does the intricate design and maintenance of homes and dams protect the beaver and its offspring, but it provides an entire ecosystem for other wildlife. In the end, this ecosystem benefits human beings.

By exploring the wonders of nature, we often come face to face with small things that fit beautifully into a grand plan—a plan that points to a Designer.

Archaeological Sites of Jesus' Crucifixion and Resurrection

They tried everything to get rid of this Christian "cult" once and for all. They had razed the city of Jerusalem in A.D. 70, when Christianity had reached a peak there. They persecuted the Christians in every corner of the Roman Empire. Each emperor faced the surge in popularity of Christianity—and the Christians who increased in number despite the horrible punishment they received. Now it was Emperor Hadrian's turn.

Hadrian, who became emperor in A.D. 117, was determined to erase the memory of Jesus—and the crucifixion and the resurrection—from the minds of the people. His tactics involved the levying of taxes on Christians and Jews in the name of pagan gods, and restricting worship practices. He also desecrated the sites of the crucifixion and the resurrection by building temples to pagan gods there. He erected a statue of Venus at the site of the crucifixion, and a statue of Jupiter at the site of the resurrection. Hadrian believed that changing the focus from Jesus to the pagan gods would ultimately cause people to "forget" the sites.

Nothing could have been further from the truth. Emperor Constantine—the emperor who finally ended persecution and made Christianity the religion of the Roman Empire—sent his mother, Helena, to mark the holy sites of Jesus' life in about 326. She quickly focused on the location of the sites of the crucifixion and resurrection, where she constructed a church to venerate them. Eusebius, the noted church historian (263–339), spoke in the church Helena constructed. He remarked that all Helena had to do was remove a small temple of Venus constructed by Hadrian in 135 over the site of the crucifixion. Not surprisingly, early Christians were well aware of the site and simply passed the knowledge of this holy place down from generation to generation using the pagan statue as a landmark. Hadrian's strategy to have Christians forget the site had backfired.

Further confirming the authenticity of the site is its location within the city walls of Helena's time, when customarily crucifixions would be outside of the city—indicating there had to be some special knowledge of the site. About 15 years after the crucifixion, King Herod Agrippa I had built a new wall extending Jerusalem's boundary on the north side. Helena would not have presumed a crucifixion would have taken place *inside* the new city boundary had she not known the exact location—which was actually *outside* the *original* boundary.

Archaeologists have found portions of the original foundation of Helena's church, which adds strong evidence of the authenticity of the sites of the crucifixion and resurrection. Naturally archaeology cannot prove the events that occurred at these sites. But it can prove that people *believed* that the events happened there. Since this belief originated close to the time of the crucifixion and resurrection, it adds credibility to the events themselves. At a minimum it confirms the existence of Jesus as recorded in the Bible.

An Inherent Belief
in God

Ever since the beginning of recorded history, human beings have had a natural belief in God. It doesn't matter when, where, or what culture or religion someone is born into, the assumption of God always exists. People have to actually intellectualize themselves into rejection of the intuitive knowledge of a Creator.

Why is this pre-programmed into human beings? Animals don't exhibit such behavior. It seems to be evidence that humans were uniquely designed to know and seek God.

The Fossil Record

Evolutionists attempt to exclude the possibility of the existence of God by proclaiming that life occurred randomly, and that new species developed by gradual changes through mutation. The discovery of a rapid "explosion" of new creatures during the Cambrian period (estimated to have started about 540 million years ago) has become an insurmountable problem for evolutionists theorizing gradual development. Even Darwin recognized this problem in his book *On the Origin of Species*, indicating that his evolution theory precluded such rapid development of new varieties.

The Cambrian fossil beds (near Cambria, Wales) reveal the abrupt appearance of all of the existing known animal phyla except two[4]—all in a space of time considered far too short for evolution to operate, even by its most ardent supporter.

Other analysis of the fossil record reveals many other major problems with theories that species evolved, most notably the many "gaps." In addition to the Cambrian problem, Darwin was also troubled by these. He theorized, however, that eventually fossils would be uncovered to fill in these gaps.

In Darwin's day there were relatively few fossils available, which perhaps justifies his theorizing. Today, though, it is estimated that virtually all of the known fossil species have been uncovered—and we still find missing links throughout all species chains. Even many leading evolutionists reluctantly acknowledge the problem of the fossil record. Noted evolutionist Stephen J. Gould stated,

> The absence of fossil evidence for intermediary stages between major transitions in organic design, indeed our inability, even in our imagination, to construct functional intermediates in many cases, has been a persistent and nagging problem for gradualistic accounts of evolution.[5]

There is one very logical and viable explanation for the gaps in the fossil record and the sudden appearance of a wide diversity of life in the Cambrian period: that the fossil record is actually evidence of creation according to the account in the Bible.

Overcoming the
Black Plague

In the 1600s, the dreaded black plague spread throughout Europe, eventually killing about 25 percent of the total population. People lived in constant fear. Panic gripped men, women, and children the minute any relative or close friend contracted the disease. Those caring for the sick were tired, overworked, and at their wits' end. They had tried everything to stop the plague's progress. Nothing was working, and people were dying everywhere. The stench of death filled the streets of the small towns and the large cities.

Finally, when all else failed, the leaders approached the clergy—asking them to help, perhaps suspecting that only divine intervention could cure the outbreak. Certainly many prayers were made. Additionally, the clergy cited the laws of Moses and several commandments of God, involving

- ❖ quarantine (Leviticus 13:45-46)

- ❖ handling of the dead (Numbers 19:11-22)

- ❖ disposal of human waste (Deuteronomy 23:12-14)

Today these principles seem obvious because we understand the germs that cause disease. However, this was not understood at the time of the black plague. By simply trusting in the inspired words of the Bible and following the above laws, the black plague was eventually overcome.

The manner in which the black plague was overcome provides evidence that the Bible was inspired by God.

Prophecies of Jesus' Betrayal

History records that Jesus was betrayed by His disciple and friend Judas Iscariot (Matthew 27:4; Mark 14:41; Luke 22:48; John 18:2). Other very interesting details of this betrayal are given, namely that it was for 30 pieces of silver (Matthew 26:14-15); that the money was thrown on the floor of the Temple (27:5); and that it was "given to a potter" (27:6-7).

At first sight, one might say, "So what?" These are simply facts, although admittedly very specific ones. Upon further investigation, we find that the pages of the Old Testament foretold all of these specific events through prophecies given hundreds of years in advance:

❖ Betrayal by a friend—prophesied 1000 years in advance.

Even my close friend, whom I trusted,
he who shared my bread,
has lifted up his heel against me.
　　　　　　　—PSALM 41:9

❖ Betrayal for 30 pieces of silver that were thrown into the house of the Lord, then given to the potter—prophesied 500 years in advance.

I told them, "If you think it best, give me my pay; but if not, keep it." So they paid me thirty pieces of silver.

And the LORD said to me, "Throw it to the potter"—the handsome price at which they priced me! So I took the thirty pieces of silver and threw them into the house of the LORD to the potter.

—ZECHARIAH 11:12-13

How were these precise prophecies made so far in advance?

Ice Floats

Water (H_2O) is more special than most people think. We know it is necessary for all life. But if water didn't behave in a unique way, much of life—certainly human life—wouldn't exist.

Consider that almost all substances contract as they get colder. Water expands and eventually freezes, causing it to float. If ice contracted and sank, like other substances, the polar ice caps would sink. Water would cover most of the livable dry land. Some years would be worse than others—and most of land life as we know it would cease to exist. Aquatic life would be drastically affected also, as sinking ice would churn up deep waters (including life there) and alter normal ocean currents, forcing marine life into an untenable environment.

This seemingly minor yet unusual aspect of water—that it floats when it freezes—is evidence of divine engineering that is actually necessary for life on earth.

The Site of Jesus' Birth

Archaeologists have identified the probable site of Jesus' birth in the city of Bethlehem, approximately five miles outside of Jerusalem. Unlike the wooden stables so often represented in commercial Christmas displays, the actual stable was almost certainly a cave, which was quite typical in the first century.

Among other things, one important consideration would lead us to the conclusion that the currently identified site is authentic. The events surrounding the birth of Jesus were dramatic and memorable. It was no ordinary birth.

1. Zechariah (John the Baptist's father) lost his ability to speak and miraculously regained it, then proclaimed his son as the forerunner to Jesus.

2. Elizabeth (John the Baptist's mother) recognized Mary as the mother of the Messiah (Luke 1:41-45).

3. Angels appeared to shepherds, who then announced the birth of Jesus around Bethlehem.

4. Simeon recognized Jesus as the Messiah (Luke 2:25-35).

5. Anna recognized Jesus as the Messiah (Luke 2:36-38).

6. Powerful magi ("wise men") with a supporting army rode into town (Matthew 2:1-12).

7. A few years later, King Herod ordered the killing of all male children two years old and under (Matthew 2:16).

In short, the birth of Jesus was anything but ordinary. It was highly memorable.

Today, even with the most ordinary of births, family and friends recall where the birth took place. Why would anyone think things were different at the time of Jesus? Add to that the many other people that were undoubtedly aware of the birth (due to the shepherds, the magi, the killings ordered by Herod), and we have a considerable number of people that would be aware of the site. Later, as the mission of Jesus was revealed through His death and resurrection, early Christian leaders marked and venerated many significant sites of Jesus' ministry. (It was not unlike the case of great leaders today, whose childhood homes are often marked.)

The ancient historian Eusebius wrote that the emperor Constantine and his mother, Helena, constructed a church over the cave of the birth of Jesus, and lavishly adorned it.[6]

As with the sites of the crucifixion and resurrection, the Roman emperor Hadrian had hoped to obscure it with a pagan symbol. In this case, a grove of trees dedicated to the god Adonis was planted around it, which only served to mark the site for future generations.

Since then several churches have been constructed on the site each over an earlier one. By excavating the historical churches, built as monuments on this site over the centuries, we can have confidence in the authenticity of Jesus' birthsite. It is fully consistent with the biblical record.

Locating the site of Jesus' birth helps confirm His existence. While it doesn't prove His claim to be God, it does help indicate that the early Christians believed He was. Archaeology helps confirm the authenticity of the Bible.

DNA: Information Stored Within Human Beings

Every cell in the body of a human being contains DNA molecules that contain the information to (a) define the individual, and (b) direct its functions.

DNA is in a *double helix* shape—like a twisted ladder. Each "rung" of the ladder is called a *base pair*—made up of chemicals that influence characteristics. Several base pairs are grouped together into *genes*, and genes are strung together into sequences. All of this defines the makeup and functions of the person. A single human DNA molecule has 3.2 billion base pairs; hence it encodes an enormous amount of information.

How vast is the information encoded in the DNA of a single human being? If all of one person's DNA were unraveled and placed end to end, it would stretch from the center of the earth to beyond the edge of the solar system!

I praise you because I am fearfully and wonderfully made;
your works are wonderful,
I know that full well.
My frame was not hidden from you

when I was made in the secret place.
When I was woven together in the depths of the earth,
your eyes saw my unformed body.
All the days ordained for me
were written in your book
before one of them came to be.
—PSALM 139:14-16

The vast complexity of 3.2 billion base pairs of information and their organization into individual characteristics is far beyond human design, even human imagination. It is evidence of design by God.

Emotions

Joy...Sorrow.
Contentment...Worry.
Confidence...Fear.
Compassion...Anger.
Love...Hate.

Emotions. You can't see them, touch them, hear them, or smell them. There is no electromagnetic, gravitational, or other scientific description for them—yet we know they exist.

Emotions have no naturalistic explanation. They add richness, depth, and meaning to life. Positive emotions such as joy, contentment, and compassion allow us to experience the most out of life. Love, the most important emotion described in the Bible, affords the opportunity to enter into a meaningful, intimate relationship with other human beings and with the God of the universe.

Often emotions are choices we make, such as the choice to love or hate. The Bible teaches that such a choice was established so that human beings might choose to love God out of our own free will.

Emotions, supernatural in origin and spiritual in existence, provide evidence of a powerful Creator beyond time, matter, and space. The Bible shows how emotions have often led people away from God. They can also lead people to God. Yet more importantly, the Bible reveals that the key emotion—the emotion of love—defines the omnipotent Creator.

Medical Principles
in the Bible

Sometimes we forget that medical practices we take for granted were not "discovered" until relatively recently. For example, sterilization was not discovered until 1865 (by Sir Joseph Lister)—which was the last year of the Civil War. The eighth day was not recognized as the ideal day for circumcision until 1947. And principles of proper waste control and quarantine were not defined until put into practice—by implementing the laws contained in the Bible during the black plague (see reason 13). Reduction of stress through many methods such as surrender to God, forgiveness, and love of others is also emphasized throughout the Bible—and has now proven to be an important medical principle.

All of the above medical practices were written in the Bible at least 3000 years before their discovery by science (Genesis 17:12; Leviticus 11–13; Deuteronomy 23; Numbers 19). One might wonder if this was by accident. Or were these wonderful medical principles truly designed by God to protect His people, as He promised? When the Hebrews were leaving Egypt after 400 years in bondage, God promised that they would have none of the diseases of the Egyptians if they followed His decrees:

> *If you listen carefully to the voice of the LORD your God and do what is right in his eyes, if you pay attention to his commands and keep all his decrees, I will not bring on you any of the diseases I brought on the Egyptians, for I am the LORD, who heals you.*
> —EXODUS 15:26

The many medical principles revealed in the Bible thousands of years before they were known to science indicates that the Bible was inspired by God.

The Monarch Butterfly

A breath of wind nudged the butterfly momentarily before it settled into the lilac for a snack. Magnificent in form and breathtaking in its vivid coloring, the monarch lived up to its name as the "king" of the insect world.

Only a few short weeks ago, the monarch had been nothing but a motionless unhatched egg. As the shell started to move and the egg began to break apart, a tiny caterpillar started to wiggle out. For four weeks it traveled the fields, looking for its daily feast of milkweed. It looked like an ugly worm—not the insect "ruler" it was destined to become. Eventually it reached full growth and began to spin a miniature "house," the *pupa* or *chrysalis*—where it underwent one of the most mysterious metamorphoses known to humans. After about two weeks, the form of the new monarch could be seen through the chrysalis's now-transparent walls.

The most dramatic moment in the monarch's life came when it broke free from the chrysalis and stretched its wings for the first time. Although wet when it emerged, the wings quickly dried, allowing the butterfly the chance to explore the world and dine on a variety of flowers as it traveled. For weeks the monarch traveled the coast, moving well over a thousand miles from California to the mountains of Mexico.

Consider the original state of the monarch. It was an uninteresting worm. Crawling on its belly, it spent all of its worm-life in the small area of a few square feet. Later, though, it emerged as a glorious "king" of the butterflies. It traveled far across the world, soaring through the air for over a thousand miles, to the peaks of mountains. Humans, too, have the hope of changing from a life of despair to a life with a spirit that soars.

And what of its change in form? The ugly worm had to "die" to its old form in order to be "born again" with a new and glorious body. Is this an example of what human death will be like?

The monarch is a testimony to the handiwork of an insightful Creator.

The House of the
Apostle Peter

Ancient pilgrims had written about the house of Peter, describing it as an octagonal church converted from the "house of the chief of the apostles." In Capernaum (a town by the Sea of Galilee that was frequented by Jesus), in 1968, the Franciscan archaeologist Virgilio Corbo began careful excavation of an octagonal structure. What he eventually found was a fifth-century church built atop a "house church" dating to the fourth century, which lay on top of a simple "courtyard house" from the first century.

One room of the house contained more than 15 invocations in Aramaic, Greek, Hebrew, Latin, and Syriac scratched into the walls. Several clues indicated that the room carried special significance to first-century Christians and was revered by later generations. Walls of the room had been replastered at least twice, and normal domestic pottery had ceased to be used in the room after the middle of the first century, indicating the room had some other special significance.

The construction of the house was typical of the city. The walls would not support a second story or a masonry roof. They would, however, support the kind of thatched roof indicated in the Bible (Mark 2:4). The continuous reverence attached to the house—with churches built on top of churches—along with continuous identification of the site as the house of Peter through the centuries, lends credence to the accuracy of the claim.

It would be natural for Christians to revere the house of Peter. This archaeological find lends credibility to the authenticity of the Bible.

The Laws of Physics

- ❖ A bridge

- ❖ A refrigerator

- ❖ An airplane

- ❖ An elevator

- ❖ A lightbulb

- ❖ A computer

- ❖ A building

All of the above are possible because of the laws of physics that have existed since the first second of the universe's existence. Certain engineering principles, like the mechanics of the wheel and the lever, were accidentally "discovered" long ago. Others, like the laws of thermodynamics or Einstein's relativity laws, were discovered relatively recently.

Yet the laws themselves show order in the universe. It's an order that governs everything from the motion of planets and the explosion of stars to the revolution of electrons around the atom's nucleus.

Ironically, laws of physics are typically used to define so-called "natural" events—sometimes even in an attempt to rule out God. Yet the remarkable precision and existence of the laws themselves speaks to their supernatural origin.

Beethoven

Where did such unique genius come from?

The Cry of a Baby

Sweat from Sharon's brow stung the corners of her eyes before pouring down the sides of her face. Her breathing was labored. She grimaced and shrieked as she was hit by another gut-wrenching spasm. The pain seemed too much to bear.

Tom, her husband, knelt by her side, helpless except for the comfort he offered through his soothing words and by holding her hand. They had had to pull the car over on a deserted road in the middle of the night, and the baby was surely due any moment.

Sharon screamed again, louder than before. Now her blouse was soaked with sweat. Fear was in her eyes.

Then she pushed with all of her might...and for a brief moment it was quiet in the cool nighttime air.

The unmistakable cry broke the silence. Tom carefully picked up the tiny newborn child. For a few tender moments he held the baby to his chest, breathing a sigh of relief. Then he gently passed the infant to Sharon.

She smiled, and a tear of joy trickled down her cheek. What a wonderful, incredible thing she held in her arms. What a gift. The couple looked into each other's eyes in silence, both thinking the same thing.

The cry of new life comes not from water or fire or rock or something dead.

It comes from God.

Infinity and a Finite Universe

Recently science has discovered that time is finite (see reason 49). Hence we can ascertain that something outside of time must have created time itself. In other words, something must have *transcended* time in order to produce it in its first finite state.

Therefore, something must exist outside of the space–time domain—which would lead to the conclusion of the necessity of an infinite God.

The Martyrdom of
the Apostles

After Jesus was crucified and rose from the dead, there was a distinct change in all of the remaining apostles (Judas had killed himself). They went from being ordinary tradesmen to being aggressive, outspoken evangelists. Why would this happen—unless Jesus had actually risen from the dead? After all, if Jesus had simply died and nothing else, His prophecy that He would rise from the dead—proving His deity—would have been false. What good would a dead Messiah be? And surely, sooner or later the corpse of Jesus would be found anyway, proving the disciples to have been fools.

But the disciples, having seen the risen Christ, were confident the corpse would never be found. And their confidence was obvious in their preaching. As persecution intensified, it became apparent that their continued evangelism would eventually cost them their lives. Instead of backing off, they preached the gospel even more aggressively. One by one they were martyred for their faith. According to historical tradition,

❖ *Peter* was crucified upside down in Nero's Circus.

❖ *James son of Zebedee* was put to death by Herod Agrippa I (Acts 12:2). His beheading inspired one of the executioners to seek Jesus.

❖ *Andrew* was crucified in Greece on a cross in the form of an X.

❖ *Thomas* was killed by a lance thrust by jealous Hindus on the slopes of Mount Antenodur.

❖ *Matthew* was pinned to the ground and beheaded for his faith.

❖ *Philip* was crucified by piercing through his thighs, then stoned.

❖ *Bartholomew (Nathaniel)* was crucified at Albana (now Derbend, Russia).

❖ *Thaddaeus* was killed by arrows on Mount Ararat.

❖ *James son of Alphaeus* was stoned to death by the Jews for preaching the gospel.

❖ *Simon the zealot* was sawn in two for preaching the gospel.

Of the 12 original disciples only John died a natural death.

All of the disciples certainly knew Jesus well and would have known whether the resurrection was true or false. One by one, over a period of many years in many different places, they endured painful martyr deaths. Each knew his time would eventually come if he continued to preach the gospel. And any one of them could have avoided a horrible death simply by stopping. Why did they insist on continuing?

When considering the choice of each of Jesus' disciples to accept a horrible martyr's death instead of renouncing Jesus, we must remember one thing that separates all of them from any martyr for any other religion. They were not dying for some philosophy or idea. They were dying because of a *historical fact*—one they would certainly know—that Jesus rose again from the dead. It is the most important historical fact of all time. A fact that proves Jesus is God.

The Complexity of
Human Beings

The cause of a thing must pre-exist the thing.
The cause of a thing must be of equal or higher complexity.
Therefore, something had to pre-exist human beings to cause them to exist. And that cause had to have been of equal or greater complexity than a human being.

The Inscription of
Pontius Pilate

Archaeologists were clearing the sand from the ruins of a theater in the Roman capital city of Caesarea Maritima (on the Mediterranean coast of present-day Israel) when they came across a stone, turned upside down, bearing the name Pontius Pilate—Roman prefect of Judea. The plaque boasted that Pilate was dedicating a newly built amphitheater to Emperor Tiberius (see Luke 3:1).[7]

Archaeologists indicate the stone was not in its original position, but had been reused in theater construction in the fourth century. It was an important find for several reasons. First, it established the existence of Pontius Pilate through archaeology (in addition to the manuscripts that have indicated his existence). Second, it settled a dispute over whether Pilate was in fact a *prefect* (governor) instead of the inferior *procurator,* as some had thought. Third, it corroborated a timing link to Tiberius Caesar. And finally, it demonstrated Pilate's desire to appeal to the graces of Tiberius in his affairs.

In summary, the stone indicates that Pontius Pilate served as the prefect of Judea at the time of Jesus. It authenticates the description provided by the Bible.

Pleasure

We crave it. We seek it. We thrive on it. Pleasure.

How wonderful it is to bite into a peach, or think about the beauty of a physically attractive human being. How pleasurable it is to look at them.

Perhaps the beautiful sounds of music reach your ears. Or you consider the act of reproduction—how pleasurable it is.

Exactly what is pleasure? Why is there pleasure? How do we measure it? Although the source of pleasurable thinking has been identified in the brain, nobody really knows what pleasure is, other than that it is something that we crave. It is beyond the laws of physics.

Pleasure encourages humans (and other animals) to do things that are necessary for survival. Couldn't such actions have arisen in DNA as instincts—but with no need to provide pleasure? Why do we *enjoy* many of the things we do to merely survive? Is it that someone wants us to experience ultimate joy?

The Contradiction of
Two Natural Laws

In 1916, Albert Einstein first expanded his theory of *special relativity* ($E = mc^2$) into *general relativity,* which essentially proposes that matter (and therefore gravity) causes space and the flow of time to curve. Since first proposed, the theory has been refined mathematically and tested experimentally to the point that now it is considered a law by many scientists, and has been proven as significant as virtually any law in physics. Perhaps the most significant result of the verification of general relativity is the "proof" that time, space, and matter had a beginning!

The first law of thermodynamics has also been proven experimentally and has been utilized as a valid law of physics for many years. The first law is the law of conservation of energy—in other words, the total energy of a system and its surroundings is constant. Matter, which is a source of latent energy (heat, fusion, and so on) is a part of the overall first law. The law indicates that the total of matter and energy in a closed system cannot be changed. Matter and energy can neither be created nor destroyed (simply converted from one form to another—like the burning of wood to create heat).

The first law of thermodynamics, which predicts that matter and energy cannot be created in a closed system (like a universe) directly contradicts Einstein's general relativity, which indicates that there was a beginning ("creation") of time, matter, and space.

How does one reconcile such a contradiction, when we know that both laws of physics are true? Only creation outside of known human dimensions could account for both.

Non-Christian Evidence
for Jesus

A number of ancient non-Christian sources refer to Jesus, and in some cases to His crucifixion, "supposed" resurrection, and miracles.

❖ *The Jewish (Babylonian) Talmud,* written in the tannaitic period (roughly 200 B.C. to A.D. 200), indicated that Jesus
    1. existed
    2. was crucified on the eve of Passover
    3. performed miracles
    4. led many away from Jewish teaching
    5. was the target of Jewish leaders' plot to kill Him

❖ *Josephus,* a first-century Jewish historian, indicated that Jesus
    1. existed
    2. was a miracle worker
    3. drew many away from the Jewish leaders
    4. was crucified, but was loyally followed anyway by His disciples

❖ *Tacitus,* a first- and second-century Roman historian, indicated that early Christians were falsely persecuted by Nero. He indicated that Jesus was put to death by Pontius Pilate, and that the Christians believed that Jesus rose from the dead.

❖ *Pliny the Younger,* a first-century governor and historian, indicated the existence of Christians and their usual, often strong, belief in the resurrection of Jesus.

❖ *Suetonius,* an early historian and secretary to the emperor Hadrian, spoke of early Christians and Jesus. He discussed the belief in the resurrection.

❖ *Phlegon,* an ancient historian, discussed the darkness and earthquakes at the time of the crucifixion—corroborating the biblical account. He also referred to prophecies that Jesus made and indicated that they had come true.

❖ *Lucian of Samosata,* an ancient satirist with a passion for truth, poked fun at Christians. Despite his rhetoric, Lucian indicated that Jesus existed, that He was known for miracles, that He was crucified, that His followers thought highly of Him and were converted from the gods of Greece, and that they "worshiped" Him.

❖ *Hadrian,* a Roman emperor known for persecuting Christians, wrote about them and the methods for testing and persecuting them.

Evidence from non-Christian sources verifies many things about Jesus, including 1) His existence, 2) His miracles, 3) His crucifixion, 4) His followers, and 5) early belief in His resurrection.

A New Body Every
Five Years

In the time it takes you to read this sentence, ten billion trillion atoms in your body have been replaced. It takes about five years for every single atom in an adult body to be replaced. The mystery is this: If every atom of every molecule in every cell in a human body is replaced every five years, how is it that we are still the same person?

❖ Why is our personality the same?

❖ Why is our character the same?

❖ How do our muscles remember such things as a golf swing or how to paint with oils?

❖ How does our mind remember things?

Apparently a person is something far beyond the mere atoms and molecules of the cells themselves. Apparently something else exists. Something supernatural. Something from God.

The Miracles of Jesus

M any miracles of Jesus have been documented by the most well-attested writing of all time—the documents of the New Testament. These miracles included the following:

- ❖ turning water into wine

- ❖ miraculous catches of fish

- ❖ casting out demons

- ❖ healing lepers

- ❖ healing paralytics

- ❖ healing a shriveled hand

- ❖ healing the lame

- ❖ healing the blind

- ❖ healing the mute

- ❖ healing the sick

- ❖ feeding thousands with just a little food

❖ calming of the sea

❖ walking on water

❖ raising people from the dead

Many people witnessed and openly acknowledged these miracles—even among the enemies of Jesus. The vastness of the early manuscript evidence, supported by the belief of early Christians who died, among other reasons, to defend the truth of Jesus' miracles, testifies to their validity.

For the skeptic, there is also non-Christian evidence—even written by His enemies—referring to Jesus' miracles. The Jewish Talmud, other early Jewish writings, and Josephus, a first-century Jewish historian, all have various indications of miracles by Jesus or healings in the name of Jesus.

The Jews thought that the miracles of Jesus were miracles that could only be performed by God. About 700 years before Jesus, Isaiah had prophesied that God would come and produce such miracles (Isaiah 35:4-6). The miracles of Jesus provide evidence that Jesus is God.

Light

Light is one of the most familiar and important, yet still mysterious, forces in the universe. The common definition of light relates to the visible spectrum of a wide range of electromagnetic energy, from very short gamma waves to very long radio waves.

As familiar as light is—having been critical to life since the beginning—scientists have yet to completely understand it. Instead, they understand its properties and how it behaves. For instance, we know that light reflects, refracts, can be diffused, and can be polarized. We know that its speed is 299,792.458 kilometers per second (in a vacuum)—faster than anything else. (While there are occasional claims about faster-than-light phenomena made by a few, most scientists regard such claims as science fiction.)

We know that light has properties of waves, with each color of the spectrum having a different wavelength. We also know that light has particle-like properties, and in experiments we can see that light particles (photons) make things move. Finally, we know light has mysterious quantum properties, which are important in the fields of atomic and molecular physics.[8]

It's interesting to recognize that this important, life-giving phenomenon exists with three separate properties—wave, particle, and quantum—all bound together in one. The Bible claims that God is made up of three persons—the Father, the Son, and the Holy Spirit—bound together in one. The Bible also says that "God is light" (1 John 1:5). Throughout the Bible, light is used as a symbol of goodness and love. Light is necessary for human existence. Perhaps light itself is an inspired, intentional model of something necessary for human existence—God.

The First-Century Fishing Boat

Droughts in Israel in the 1980s caused great hardship to the people and caused the water level of the Sea of Galilee to drop significantly. However, the receding water exposed a well-preserved first-century fishing boat in the mud not far from the new shoreline. Under the direction of the Israel Antiquities Authority, archaeologists began a race against time to carefully extract the boat from the mud before the waters returned. A complex system of dikes and hydraulics was set up to slowly raise the boat. Eventually it was placed in a climate-controlled environment to protect it from aging.

The fishing boat was of the type described in the Gospels:

> One day Jesus said to his disciples, "Let's go over to the other side of the lake." So they got into a boat and set out. As they sailed, he fell asleep. A squall came down on the lake, so that the boat was being swamped, and they were in great danger.
>
> The disciples went and woke him, saying, "Master, Master, we're going to drown!"

He got up and rebuked the wind and the raging waters; the storm subsided, and all was calm. "Where is your faith?" he asked his disciples.

In fear and amazement they asked one another, "Who is this? He commands even the winds and the water, and they obey him."

—LUKE 8:22-25

Pots and lamps found inside the boat dated it to the first century. Carbon-14 testing further confirmed the dating. The design of the boat was typical of fishing boats used during that period on the Sea of Galilee. In the back of the boat was a raised section like the one where Jesus could have been sleeping, as indicated in the Gospel accounts. The boat could accommodate 15 people including crew. This archaeological discovery confirms the description given in the Bible.

Electron–Proton Mass Ratio: Perfect for Life

Hardly anyone thinks of the ratio of the mass of protons and electrons in atoms—except for theoretical physicists. Yet this ratio is one of the most fundamental and important ratios in all existence.

Physicists indicate that a proton is 1836 times more massive than an electron. If this ratio varied only slightly, the required molecules for life would not form—there would be no chemistry and no life at all.

Did this precise ratio of atomic particles come about by accident? After all, it could have been any number at all. It is so amazing that even an agnostic physicist, the esteemed "Newton's chair" professor Stephen Hawking, believes it is almost beyond coincidence. He notes, "The remarkable fact is that the values of these numbers seem to have been very finely adjusted to make possible the development of life."[9]

How did such a fundamental ratio of atoms become so "finely adjusted"?

The Amazing
Timed Collision

Scientists are fairly certain that a heavenly body about half the size of Mars collided with the Earth at precisely the right time in the Earth's development. This collision "knocked" much of the carbon dioxide (CO_2) out of the atmosphere, averting a life-preventing "runaway greenhouse effect" and allowing the right atmospheric chemistry. It also increased the speed of the earth's rotation (another crucial factor). The moon was formed from part of the colliding body, and it became a vital element in stabilizing the earth's axis and rotation, thus creating the environment for life. How did such a unique event happen in such a precise way to help make Earth perfect for human beings?

Sir William Ramsay

Sir William Ramsay was one of the most skilled archaeologists of his day. He had rejected much of the written New Testament account and was determined to prove it false based on other writings of the day that contradicted the Bible.

He set out to prove the historian Luke wrong, hoping to confirm what many archaeologists had once thought—that the Bible was full of errors. Ramsay believed that the books of Luke and Acts had actually been written in about A.D. 150 and therefore did not bear the authenticity that a first-century document would have. His archaeological journeys took him to 32 countries, 44 cities, and 9 islands.[10] After some 15 years of intensive study, he concluded, "Luke is a historian of the first rank—this author should be placed along with the very greatest of historians." Ramsay himself is regarded as one of the greatest archaeologists of all time.

Archaeologists in the nineteenth century thought the Bible was full of errors. Some popular misconceptions that Ramsay helped correct are as follows:

❖ *Critics thought* that there was no Roman census as indicated in Luke 2:1.

- *Ramsay discovered* there was a Roman census every 14 years beginning with Emperor Augustus.

❖ *Critics thought* that Quirinius was not governor of Syria at the time of Jesus' birth as indicated in Luke 2:2.

  - *Ramsay discovered* that Quirinius was governor of Syria in about 7 B.C.

❖ *Critics thought* that people did not have to return to their ancestral home as indicated in Luke 2:3.

  - *Ramsay discovered* that people did have to return to their home city—verified by an ancient Egyptian papyrus giving directions for conducting a census.

❖ *Critics questioned* the existence of the treasurer of the city of Corinth, Erastus (Romans 16:23).

  - *Ramsay discovered* a city pavement in Corinth bearing the inscription "Erastus, curator of public buildings, laid this pavement at his own expense."

❖ *Critics thought* that Luke's reference to Gallio as proconsul of Achaia was wrong (Acts 18:12).

  - *Ramsay discovered* the Delphi inscription, which reads, "As Lucius Junius Gallio, my friend and proconsul of Achaia..."

Time and time again Ramsay's search to find evidence that Luke's writing was in error turned up evidence that it was, in fact, accurate. As a result, Ramsay eventually converted to Christianity. His archaeological research added strong support for the authenticity of the Bible.

Blood: The Source of Life

Oxygen is vital to help provide energy to every living cell. In fact, cells can't go for long without it. Considering that there are between 10 and 100 trillion cells in a human body, how can our body possibly provide the necessary oxygen in a relatively short period of time?

First we breathe in oxygen, which in the lungs comes in contact with capillary walls that—due to a favorable diffusion factor—allow the oxygen into the bloodstream. However, oxygen doesn't dissolve well into the bloodstream itself. It does, however, dissolve extremely well into the hemoglobin in the tiny red blood cells in the bloodstream. The red blood cells are the vehicles that deliver the oxygen throughout the body, via tiny capillaries that at times are only the width of a single red blood cell.

The network of blood vessels and capillaries is vast—in fact a human body contains about 60,000 miles of them.[11] This is enough to circle the earth two-and-a-half times. The number of red blood cells within this system is also vast—they would circle the earth four times if placed end to end. Since each individual red blood cell can hold as many as one million oxygen molecules, and since each cell returns about once a minute to be replenished with oxygen at the lungs, there is adequate oxygen for the body.

Could the circulatory system have happened by random chance? First, there are many individual parts to the system that require other parts to function. Therefore, these parts could not have developed sequentially—independently—since any single part would have been of no value by itself. All parts were necessary at once.

Second, just the odds of the random lining up of the correct amino acids for the hemoglobin portion of the red blood cell are roughly 1 chance in 10^{850}![12] This is essentially a zero possibility of random development. For example, it would be like breaking all the atoms in the universe into subatomic particles and correctly selecting a single marked one by chance...not once, not twice, but ten times over!

The Bible recognized that blood really is the source of life nearly 1500 years before Christ: "The life of a creature is in the blood" (Leviticus 17:11).

Therefore, modern understanding of the circulatory system and the red blood cells within our body help confirm the existence of the Creator, and also that the Bible is inspired by God.

The Professor's Mind

A philosophy professor proclaimed there was no God. He reasoned that God was impossible because He couldn't be observed through any of the five senses.

A student stood up and asked the professor if any student could see, touch, taste, smell, or feel the professor's mind. The professor replied, "Of course not."

"Based on the logic you have taught us to use," the student replied, "if there is no God because we can't use our five senses to detect Him, then one would likewise be compelled to conclude that you have no mind."

No one argues that one's own mind does not exist. Logically, then, there is no reason to exclude the existence of God.

The Hydrologic Cycle

Water runs down mountains and hills into lakes, and eventually to the ocean, providing life to the multitude of creatures all along the journey. Then it evaporates into clouds, which begin their own journey. Whisked over oceans, plains, deserts, and mountains the clouds travel until they are cooled enough to condense into rain. Life-giving water then again runs into rivers, lakes, and streams, and the whole process starts all over again.

This is the hydrologic cycle. Today we take it for granted. However, the process wasn't clearly recognized by science until Perrault and Mariotte identified it in the 1700s.

This system seems designed specifically to provide an essential for life everywhere—to everything that needs it. Clouds blown over the surface of the earth provide water to virtually every part of the planet. There is nothing else that behaves like this "water delivery system" on a mass scale.

The Bible correctly referred to the hydrologic cycle over 3000 years ago:

> *He draws up the drops of water,*
> *which distill as rain to the streams;*
> *the clouds pour down their moisture.*
> —Job 36:27-28

All streams flow into the sea,
yet the sea is never full.
To the place the streams come from,
there they return again.
—ECCLESIASTES 1:7

The hydrologic system is miraculously designed to serve the needs of everything on planet Earth. It indicates a Supreme Designer—God—and the biblical references thousands of years in advance indicate that the Bible was inspired by God.

Ancient New Testament Manuscripts

What kind of "proof" do human beings demand for one-time events, such as a robbery, a murder—or a resurrection? *Legal* evidence. This evidence is obtained from such things as eyewitness testimony and circumstantial evidence.

The written record of the New Testament—especially the Gospel accounts—provides the best source of eyewitness testimony for the events of Jesus' time. Scholars generally agree that all of the autographs—original manuscripts—of this testimony were written within 25 to 60 years of Jesus' death at the latest (see reason 78). They were widely copied and circulated within the time of the eyewitnesses. Therefore, if there were any key contradictions of the truth, they could have easily been challenged by those knowing the facts. Any false Gospel accounts would not have withstood such intense scrutiny—especially when so many lives depended on its accuracy during the time of persecution.

The credibility and accuracy of these eyewitness accounts depends primarily on two criteria: 1) the number of comparative manuscripts and the consistency between them, and 2) the length of time from the autograph to the copies of manuscripts. In both of these criteria, the New Testament demonstrates a degree of accuracy far above other ancient works that have been deemed reliable and historical. Consider the following list[13] of ancient works, the number of copies, and the elapsed time from the autograph to the earliest copy:

Author and document	Number of manuscripts	Proximity of earliest copy to autograph (years)
Homer's *Iliad*	643	400
Herodotus' *History*	8	1350
Thucydides' *History*	8	1300
Plato	7	1300
Demosthenes	200	1400
Caesar's *Gallic Wars*	10	1000
Livy's *History of Rome*	1 partial,	400
	19 copies	1000
Tacitus' *Annals*	20	1000
Pliny Secundus' *History*	7	750
New Testament	5366	50 to 225 years

Of course the plethora of existing New Testament documents represents a minuscule fraction of those that were created. During the persecution, ancient Bibles were burned and people found with Bibles were executed. Yet many Bibles not only survived, but they survived in numbers far surpassing any work in history.

The length of time between the autograph and the earliest copies of the New Testament is also amazingly short—far shorter than other ancient works. This limits the amount of time that would allow errors to creep in. And finally, the consistency among the many copies is incredible. Biblical scholars who have analyzed New Testament documentation proclaim it far "purer" than that of any other book of antiquity. Scholars Norman Geisler and William Nix conclude that the New Testament has survived in a "form that is 99.5 percent pure."[14]

In summary, the vast numbers of New Testament manuscripts provide substantial legal evidence that the resurrection of Jesus was historically accurate as recorded in the Bible.

WMAP Confirms Creation Event

The Wilkinson Microwave Anisotropy Probe (WMAP—a satellite) measures data from the cosmological radiation left over from the origin of the universe. It is amazingly accurate and has enabled scientists to calculate the age of the universe to be 13.7 billion years old, plus or minus only 0.1 billion years.[15] But the important issue is not the actual age, but the proof that the universe had a beginning—just as indicated in Genesis 1:1. Limiting the time (whether to only 10,000 years or to 13.7 billion) proves that there is not nearly enough time for random evolution of the first living cell to happen (see reason 2).

The space probe also indicated that *light separated from darkness* approximately 0.00038 billion years after the creation event. This confirms the second stage of creation as indicated in Genesis 1:3 (see reason 53).

Also significant are confirmations of two precise cosmological parameters necessary for life: 1) that the mass density of the universe can differ by no more than one part in 10^{60}, and 2) that space density can differ by no more than one part in 10^{120}. This means that the universe had to be incredibly "fine-tuned" in order to be suitable for life. In order to understand how very precise these numbers are, we should understand that there are only about 10^{82} subatomic particles (that is, protons, electrons, neutrons, quarks, and so on) in the entire universe. Thus, the odds of the coincidental occurrence of the universe having both exact densities required for life would be far, far less than those of randomly selecting a "marked" electron out of the entire universe—twice in a row!

Love

What causes people to love others so much that they would die in their place? God.

And God loves people so much He would die for them too.

"Whoever does not love does not know God, because God is love" (1 John 4:8).

The Eye

The eye is an incredible piece of machinery.[16]
After light passes through the lens, it hits the retina, where light-sensitive cells convert the information into "pictures" for the brain to interpret. All of this takes place in a few picoseconds—and it takes place in 127 million rods and cones on each eye. This process is continuous and cannot be stopped even if we wanted to.

The sensitivity of the eye is astounding. The retina's photocells require only about 1 to 2 photons to trigger a visual signal. (Compare this to a flashlight, which emits about 10^{18} photons per second.) The eye can perceive a continuous range of color, yet distinguish between minute differences in shades. Adaptation of the eye affords "night vision," when images are reduced to black and white (rods predominate in activity)—and full "bright vision," when vivid colors can be seen (cones predominate in activity).

Evolutionists, trying to exclude God, would have us believe that the eye somehow gradually developed. However, upon logical analysis, this is inconceivable. Why? It's because the eye is an *irreducibly complex* system. *Irreducible complexity* is the term given to a system that requires all of the parts to be available at the same time to function. In other words, the eye requires the cornea, iris, pupil, lens, muscles, rods, cones, nerves, brain, and many other parts—all available at the same time—to function. If the eye had evolved, this process would have required each of the parts to gradually form until the eye itself would be finally in place as a fully functioning entity. However, there would be no reason or benefit for such things as a muscle or lens to form by themselves with no overall plan. What would a partial eye do? What would cause it to be preserved? What would cause gradually formed parts to miraculously assemble in the precise manner necessary to function as a whole?

When we consider its precision and complexity, and the need for all its parts to function together in order to perform, it is apparent that the eye was designed. Gradual, naturalistic evolution is impossible. Who could possibly design such a thing?

A Prophecy of Jesus' Miracles

The Jewish religious leaders believed there were miracles that could only be accomplished by God Himself. They were prophesied in the Hebrew Scriptures (the Old Testament):

> *"Be strong, do not fear;*
> *your God will come,*
> *he will come with vengeance;*
> *with divine retribution*
> *he will come to save you."*

> *Then will the eyes of the blind be opened*
> *and the ears of the deaf unstopped.*
> *Then will the lame leap like a deer,*
> *and the mute tongue shout for joy.*
> —Isaiah 35:4-6

These were some of the most common miracles Jesus performed (see reason 33). Many people who saw them believed that Jesus was who He claimed to be—God.

This prophecy, accurately recorded in the Bible hundreds of years before Jesus came, indicates that the Bible was inspired by God.

Ants

Ants go about their business much like humans. They are social. The workers, all of which are female, have specific tasks and can communicate with each other about things such as where food is and what is dangerous. Like humans, ants can cooperate with each other one minute and fight with each other the next. They live in highly organized societies that build elaborate mazelike homes. The process of building the enormous "ant castles" involves an unknown division of labor that defies logic and would be impressive on a human organizational scale. Within a period of only four to five days, a colony of about 5000 ants can move some 40 pounds of sand to develop the intricate tunnels for their home. Ants have astounding strength which allows them to accomplish this. A single ant has a relative strength six times greater than that of a cat.[17]

Apart from social and engineering skills, ants resemble humans in many ways. They care for young larvae by feeding and washing them. There is a strict caste structure. The youngest ants take care of newly hatched eggs. Middle-aged ants do most of the nesting chores. And the oldest ants do the dangerous duty of foraging for and collecting food. Apart from humans, ants are the only creatures known that invade other colonies and take slaves for their own work. Communication among ants appears to be chemical in nature. Special glands secrete chemicals that create a path for other ants to follow—for example, in the process of retrieving food for the colony.

Ants are a society that is interdependent. This interdependence combined with such complexity of individual design could not have come about gradually or by chance. All of this points to a supernatural Creator.

Inscriptions on Ossuaries

Ossuaries are small (usually about 15 inches wide by 30 inches long) containers for the bones of deceased individuals. They were an integral part of the burial practices of first-century Jews in the area of Jerusalem, where burial space was limited and costly.

The Jewish burial ritual involved placing the corpse on a bench-like ledge or carved recess in a tomb for a year. At that point, when the flesh had decomposed, the bones were transferred to the more space-efficient ossuaries. These "bone boxes" sometimes contained engravings or other markings that can provide important historical information.

References to Jesus on Jerusalem Ossuaries

The discovery of two ossuaries outside of Jerusalem in 1945 by Eleazar Sukenik provides interesting insight into first-century Christians. The ossuaries are marked with graffiti and four crosses. The words *"Iesous iou"* were found—which essentially means, "Jesus, help." Also found were the words *"Iesous aloth"*—which essentially means, "Jesus, let him arise."[18]

Experts date the ossuaries to about A.D. 50, which would have been within 20 years of Jesus' death and resurrection. Certainly there would have been many eyewitnesses to the events in Jerusalem still alive at that time. Possibly, even those who had carved the ossuaries were eyewitnesses.

The writing and crosses supply

- confirmation of the crucifixion of Jesus

- confirmation of the belief that Jesus had some power to provide resurrection

- confirmation that Jesus could perform miracles

This archaeological discovery helps verify the claim of Jesus to be God.

The Ossuary of James

One of the greatest recent archaeological discoveries is the finding of what appears to be an ossuary of James, the first leader of the church in Jerusalem and the brother of Jesus.[19]

This ossuary is unique because of its Aramaic inscription, which reads, "James, son of Joseph, brother of Jesus." Although skeptics may question whether, in fact, the Joseph and Jesus are those mentioned in the New Testament, it is highly unlikely that they are not. No one questions that the names James, Joseph, and Jesus were in common usage at the time of the first century. However, the odds of having all three names precisely fit a father and two brothers by chance would be very low—especially when one considers that no other brothers were listed. There would have to be a special reason why only one brother were listed (unless Jesus was the only other male child). In the case of James, there would have been special significance attached to Jesus, so mentioning Jude and the other brothers would diminish the focus on Him.

Additionally, it was almost unheard of to mention a brother on an ossuary at all. It would indicate that the brother was especially important or famous.

Despite a long history of archaeological forgeries in Israel, and despite ongoing dispute over it, this ossuary gives many indications of being genuine:

❖ The grammar and script of the writing fits normal usage of the period before the destruction of Jerusalem in A.D. 70.

❖ Laboratory tests reveal no traces of modern elements on the ossuary.

❖ Analysis under electron microscope shows no indication of modern tooling used in formation of any letters or decoration.

❖ There is evidence of *patina,* even in the recesses of the inscription. (Patina is a microscopic film that can only be developed over many centuries in a cave or a tomb.)

❖ Experts from the Israeli government have confirmed that "there is no evidence of modern tinkering" or forgery.

In summary, the ossuary of James provides strong support for the existence of Jesus, James, and their relationship as indicated in the Bible.

The Ossuary of Caiaphas

In November 1990, construction workers in a section south of Jerusalem's Old City broke through into a burial cave that had been sealed since Rome had destroyed the city in A.D. 70. Inside they found an ornately decorated ossuary.[20]

But this ossuary was no ordinary find. Etched on the side in Aramaic was the name *Caiaphas*. That inscription, along with other inscriptions of family members in the tomb, makes it clear that this is the actual ossuary of Caiaphas, the high priest who sought to kill Jesus:

> *The chief priests and the elders of the people assembled in the palace of the high priest, whose name was Caiaphas, and they plotted to arrest Jesus in some sly way and kill him.*
>
> —MATTHEW 26:3-4

Caiaphas was not only instrumental in leading the plot to kill Jesus, he actually presided over the trial, in which Jesus was convicted—by His own confession—of the capital offense of blasphemy.

> *The high priest [Caiaphas] said to him, "I charge you under oath by the living God: Tell us if you are the Christ, the Son of God."*
>
> *"Yes, it is as you say," Jesus replied. "But I say to all of you: In the future you will see the Son of Man sitting at the right hand of the Mighty One and coming on the clouds of heaven."*
>
> *Then the high priest tore his clothes and said, "He has spoken blasphemy! Why do we need any more witnesses? Look, now you have heard the blasphemy. What do you think?"*
>
> *"He is worthy of death," they answered.*
>
> —MATTHEW 26:63-66

The ossuary of Caiaphas provides evidence of the accuracy of the Bible.

The Big Bang and Time

The *big bang* is the term given to the model of the beginning of the universe that theorizes it came into existence from an extremely dense, small amount of mass, which then "exploded" into the heavens we witness today. The model itself does not attempt to explain whether this came about randomly or through divine planning. However, scientific support (a portion of which is known as the *anthropic principle*—see reason 88) indicates that the preparation of the universe for humanity and life was divine in nature.

As soon as experimental evidence confirmed the big-bang equations, atheist astronomer Geoffrey Burbidge worried that his atheist–evolutionist peers might embrace God and rush off to join the "First Church of Christ of the Big Bang."[21] The reason is that the big-bang model of the universe supports many biblical claims regarding God.

Time Had a Beginning

First, it indicates a *beginning of time,* which is supported by several references in the Bible:

> *In the beginning…*
>
> —GENESIS 1:1

> *...faith and knowledge resting on the hope of eternal life, which God, who does not lie, promised before the beginning of time.*
> —TITUS 1:2-3

How can time have a beginning? To us it seems as though there had to have been time before the beginning of time.

Yet how could time be endless? Didn't it have to have a beginning?

This paradox seems irreconcilable. However, this problem can be solved using mathematics and tested with experimental physics. This is the case with the issue of time.

Today, after millions of data points of testing, Einstein's theory of general relativity is deemed to be essentially a law. And general relativity indicates that time indeed had a beginning—just as indicated in Genesis 1:1.

Matter Had a Beginning

Second, the big-bang model indicates there was a *beginning of matter.* The Bible says that God *created* all matter. *Bara,* the Hebrew word used to indicate that creation of something out of nothing, is used seven times in the Bible (Genesis 1:1; 2:3; 2:4; Psalm 148:5; Isaiah 40:26; 42:5; 45:18), for example:

> *God blessed the seventh day and made it holy, because on it he rested from all the work of creating that he had done.*
> —GENESIS 2:3

> *This is what the LORD says—he who created the heavens...*
> —ISAIAH 45:18

As with time, it seems inconceivable that there could have been space with no matter, and then space *with* matter. Even the first law of thermodynamics contradicts this—yet this is precisely what general relativity has verified.

The Heavens Were Stretched Out

Third, the big-bang model also indicates both a *continual "stretching out" of the heavens* and a *completed "creation element of the necessary laws of physics,"* both of which are apparent in the Bible.

Eleven times, five different writers of the Bible indicate this "stretching out" (Job 9:8; Psalm 104:2; Isaiah 40:22; 42:5; 44:24; 45:12; 48:13; 51:13; Jeremiah 10:12; 51:15; and Zechariah 12:1). In seven of these cases, the grammatical construction implies a continuous stretching of the universe, and in the other five it implies a state of completion, or "establishment" (as in the case of the laws required for the big bang). For example:

> *He sits enthroned above the circle of the earth,*
> *and its people are like grasshoppers.*
> *He stretches out the heavens like a canopy,*
> *and spreads them out like a tent to live in.*
> —ISAIAH 40:22

> *This is the word of the Lord concerning Israel.*
> *The Lord, who stretches out the heavens, who*
> *lays the foundation of the earth, and who forms*
> *the spirit of man within him.*
> —ZECHARIAH 12:1

It's ironic that some equate the big bang with scientific evidence against God. In fact, it's the opposite. The big bang model actually supports the words of the Bible. In fact, the big-bang is one of the strongest pieces of evidence for the Bible's creation account, and for God.

Mothers

It was ten o'clock on a Saturday morning. Startled by a loud scream just outside the front door, the mother rushed out to see what was happening.

On the sidewalk she saw her five-year-old son, Justin, sprawled out on the ground, screaming and clutching his knee, which was badly scraped. Two other kids were standing there laughing at her little boy. He had just tried riding a two-wheeler for the first time. She didn't know if her son's screams were more because of the pain of the knee scrape or the laughs of his six-year-old friends, James and Michael.

"What happened?" she asked.

"Awww, Justin just can't ride a bike," Michael blurted out. "He was on only two seconds and—baaaaam!—he fell over."

"Yeah, he was braggin' about how good a rider he was," added James. "Guess that goes to show you Justin isn't ready to hang with us yet."

"So being a good bike rider is what it takes to hang out with you, huh?" Justin's mom asked.

"Kinda," said Michael. "'Cause we're cool."

"Did you know Justin's cool too?" she replied "In fact, he's already a Super-Ranger on his new Toggleman game. Have either of you reached that level yet?"

"Uh…no," replied James.

"I have an idea," said Michael. "Maybe we can help Justin learn how to ride a two-wheeler if he can help us with Toggleman."

"Sounds good to me," said Justin's mom as the four of them went into the house. After fixing his scraped knee and giving him a secret kiss the other boys couldn't see, she made a bowl of popcorn for the three boys, who were sitting down for an hour of Toggleman.

Mothers always seem to know how to do the right thing at the right time. Whether it's comforting a child who has hurt himself or herself, helping a child through emotional difficulty, or even helping a child make friends, mothers seem to intuitively know what to do. They care. How is it that mothers have these instincts?

Gravity

We can't see it.
We can't hear it.
We can't taste it.
We can't smell it.
We can't touch it.

Yet we know beyond a shadow of a doubt that it exists. No one questions the existence of gravity, because we can measure its effect on things. We can calculate its force. Recently, scientists have concluded that gravity moves much like light. And scientists have also measured its speed—it travels at (or very close to) the speed of light.[22]

Gravity is a mystery beyond imagination. The Bible speaks of the relationship of God and light (1 John 1:5). Is there a relationship between God and gravity too? Like light, gravity appears to have been made by a Creator beyond time and space.

The Dead Sea Scrolls

Perhaps the single most important archaeological find ever is the discovery of about 800 scrolls in the caves at Qumran on the northwest shore of the Dead Sea in Israel. These scrolls were written from about 250 B.C. to about A.D. 65 and were discovered by accident in 1947. The scrolls varied in condition from complete and nearly perfect to heavily damaged—broken into thousands of fragments. In addition to many scrolls relevant to the current culture, a copy of every book of the Old Testament, except Esther, was found as listed below:

Book (in order of Hebrew canon)	Number of copies (? = possible fragment)[23]
Genesis	18 + 3?
Exodus	18
Leviticus	17
Numbers	12
Deuteronomy	31 + 3?
Joshua	2
Judges	3
1 and 2 Samuel	4

1 and 2 Kings	3
Isaiah	22
Jeremiah	6
Ezekiel	7
The Twelve (the minor prophets)	10 + 1?
Psalms	39 + 2?
Proverbs	2
Job	4
Song of Songs	4
Ruth	4
Lamentations	4
Ecclesiastes	3
Esther	0
Daniel	8 + 1?
Ezra–Nehemiah	1
1 and 2 Chronicles	1

The scrolls found at Qumran had been stored deep in cave libraries by the Essenes when the Romans were advancing to crush the Jewish revolt that started in A.D. 66 (Jerusalem and the Temple were totally destroyed in the year 70, and Jews were expelled from the city). The Essenes were a sect of pious Jews that had chosen to live in seclusion apart from the religious mainstream in Jerusalem. They had developed a home at an enclave in the town of Qumran on the northwest side of the Dead Sea. There they practiced strict adherence to the Jewish religion and engaged in devoted copying of Holy Scripture. Copies of Scripture and of important Essene documents were stored in pottery jars, then placed in caves. In the year 68, when news of the advancing

Romans was received by the Essenes, the caves were abandoned. They remained untouched for nearly 1900 years.

In March 1947, a Bedouin shepherd boy named Muhammad was looking for a lost goat in the hills around Qumran. He tossed a rock into a cave and was surprised to hear the shattering of pottery. Investigating the noise, he entered the dark cave and climbed down to where a number of clay jars were stored. They contained leather scrolls wrapped in linen cloth. Because the scrolls had been so carefully prepared and sealed in the clay jars, they were in excellent condition. In the following years, other caves were found containing additional scrolls—bringing the final number to several hundred, with thousands of fragments that are still being analyzed and pieced together.

The importance of the Dead Sea scrolls can not be overstated in regard to corroborating the accuracy of the biblical manuscripts. For example, a scroll of Isaiah written in 150 B.C. in nearly perfect condition, was compared to a Masoretic Hebrew text from A.D. 916 and found to be consistent despite the 1000-year difference. In fact, only 17 *letters* showed any possible signs of change. And in the case of the letters in question, the changes represent matters of spelling and style, such as conjunctions, which would have no bearing whatsoever on the meaning of the text.

Hence, the discovery of the Dead Sea scrolls and the comparison of their text with later copies have verified beyond the shadow of a doubt that the Old Testament has accurately been handed down for centuries.

The importance of the accuracy of the Old Testament is of immeasurable importance in evaluating the truth and relevance of Jesus. This is because the Old Testament contains many ancient prophecies about the Messiah, which were fulfilled precisely by Jesus.

The scrolls, which were copies of prophecies made hundreds of years before Jesus, were themselves written decades, even centuries before Jesus. Hence we know the prophecies were not written "after the fact." This knowledge is essential in evaluating the significance of fulfillment of the prophecies by Jesus. When we analyze the statistical odds of so many prophecies coming true in any one man by mere chance, we find it to be virtually impossible without divine intervention.

The Dead Sea scrolls demonstrate the reliability of the Bible and indicate that the Old Testament prophecies were not contrived. All this leads us to the conclusion that Jesus is God.

The Bible's Account of Creation in Genesis

O nce we understand that random chance evolution has no chance of explaining the origin of life (see reason 2)—or even if we merely accept that creation is possible—a reasonable question follows: What was the process of creation? Does it agree with the Bible?

Understanding chapter 1 in the book of Genesis requires a consideration of the original Hebrew text. For example, the English translation of verse 16 might lead us to infer that the sun and moon were created on day four, after the formation of plants—a problem because the sun is necessary for plant survival. Also, how can there be "days" if there is no sun? However, the actual Hebrew used in conjunction with the words of verse 1 indicates that the sun and moon "became visible" from the surface of the earth on day four (but were previously created).

Reviewing the order of events of creation shows that the Bible is accurate as far as science can verify *for all elements the Bible records* (not all aspects of creation are listed, such as the creation of the dinosaurs). Presumably, events that are not listed have little importance for humans' interaction with their environment or for their relationship with God. It's important also to notice the vantage point (frame of reference): God's spirit was "hovering over waters" (verse 2).

The Bible's order of the events of creation agrees precisely with the order of events that scientists have confirmed:

1. *Heavenly bodies were created (verse 1).* The earth was initially covered with a thick layer of gas and dust, not allowing light to penetrate. This is probably a standard condition of planets of the earth's mass and temperature. The initial conditions described in the Bible are accepted by science: dark, formless, and void.

2. *"Let there be light" (verse 3).* The atmosphere became translucent to allow some light to reach the surface of the water—a critical prerequisite for the introduction of life (and the process of photosynthesis).

3. *Development of the hydrologic cycle (verse 6).* The "perfect" conditions of temperature, pressure, and distance from the sun would allow all forms of H_2O (solid, liquid, and vapor)—all necessary for life.

4. *Formation of land and sea (verses 9-10).* Seismic and volcanic activity occur in the precise manner to allow 30 percent of the surface to become and remain land. Scientists have determined this is the ideal ratio to promote the greatest diversity of life-forms.

5. *Creation of vegetation (verse 11).* Light, water, and large amounts of carbon dioxide set the stage for vegetation. This was the first life-form.

6. *Atmospheric transparency (verse 14)*. Plants gradually produced oxygen to a level of 21 percent. This (and other factors) caused a transparent atmosphere to form and permitted "lights in the heavens" to become visible at the surface of the earth...marking the day and night and seasons.

7. *Creation of small sea animals and birds (verse 20)*. Scientists agree these were the first animal life-forms of all classes discussed in the Bible.

8. *Creation of land animals (verse 24)*. The final life-forms created prior to humans were quadrupeds and rodents.

9. *Creation of man (verse 26)*—Final life-form created on earth.

10. *No additional creation (2:2)*. No unique creation has occurred since.

Moses wrote the account of creation nearly 1500 years before Christ. At that time there was no scientific knowledge about how the universe was created—though there were many outlandish myths. Just correctly stating the ten steps is a miracle in itself.

However, suppose Moses somehow had the ten steps. What would be the odds of simply randomly guessing the correct order? It would be about 1 chance in 4 million—roughly the odds of winning a state lottery.

Volcanoes and Earthquakes: Perfect for Life

To allow life as we know it, there had to be a precise development of planet Earth, including specific timing of increased volcanic activity and plate tectonics (movements of the earth—earthquakes).[24] Critical for the proper timing of volcanoes and tectonics is an exact amount of the radioactive elements uranium and thorium in the earth's crust.[25] Because of the rate of decline of uranium and thorium in the universe, the sun and planet Earth had to have been formed during a very small window of time in the development of the universe in order for life to exist.

Also necessary for human life is the degree of species destruction that such volcanic and tectonic activity causes[26]—which is now visible to us in the fossil record.

How did these ancient events occur in such an organized manner to properly set the stage for mankind?

Life Implies Purpose

L ife exists. And life has never come from non-life. Therefore, there must have been a first cause of life. That cause of life must have had a purpose. And some superior being must have created that purpose. Would not that superior being be God?

Miraculous Mental Abilities

The human brain is an amazing organ. It consists of 10 to 100 billion neurons, which, if stretched end to end, would circle the earth four times. These neurons make about a thousand trillion computations per second. Aside from thoughts, this involves many things we don't think about—the beating of the heart, digestion of food, and so on.

The capacity of the brain is enormous. If the brain's information were written in books and stacked, the stack would soar 500 miles into space.[27]

While the operation of an average person's brain is amazing in and of itself, sometimes the aberrations of certain people emphasize the usually unrevealed potential of this remarkable organ. The following are examples of people who have severe mental deficiencies but also have incredible mental abilities. They are known as *autistic savants,* sometimes called "islands of intelligence":

> George and Charles, identical twins, are calendar calculators. Give them a date and they can give you the day of the week over a span of eighty thousand years—forty thousand backward or

forty thousand forward. Ask them to name in which years of the next 200 (or any 200) Easter will fall on March 23 and they will name those years with lightning rapidity. They cannot count to thirty, but they swap twenty-digit prime numbers for amusement.

Leslie is blind, is severely mentally handicapped, has cerebral palsy, and has never had any formal musical training. Yet, in his teens, upon hearing Tchaikovsky's Piano Concerto No. 1 for the first time, he played it back on the piano flawlessly and without hesitation.

Jedediah has a mental age of ten and is unable to write his name. When asked the question: "In a body whose three sides are 23,145,789 yards, 5,642,732 yards, and 54,965 yards, how many cubicle 1/8ths of an inch exist?" He provided the correct twenty-eight-digit figure after a five-hour computation. "Would you like the answer backwards or forwards?"[28]

How could such characteristics of the brain come about?

The Tomb of Lazarus

In an area of ancient tombs outside the town of Bethany, less than two miles to the northeast of Jerusalem, lies the probable tomb of Lazarus—whom Jesus raised from the dead only days before He was to be crucified. Twenty-four uneven steps lead down to a small antechamber and into the eight-foot-square chamber where the body of Jesus' friend lay.

The authentic tomb of Lazarus has been preserved almost from the day of his resurrection. Early Christians passed information about the site down through generations until the time of the historian Eusebius, who, writing in about A.D. 330, described the tomb in his *Onomasticon*. He said of an area outside Bethany, "There the place of Lazarus is still shown." In 333, a guide pointed out—to the pilgrim of Bordeaux—the "crypt" where Lazarus had been lain to rest. And Jerome, writing in 390, told of a church that had been constructed near the site of the tomb of Lazarus.[29] Today, remains of the original church have been unearthed.

Knowing the location of the tomb of Lazarus doesn't prove that Jesus raised him from the dead. However, it does prove that the early Christians believed that Lazarus was a real person and that they believed in the event itself. The archaeological discovery of the tomb of Lazarus helps confirm the authenticity of the Bible.

Personal Experience

Liesl: An atheist, she was brought up in a haunted house by an alcoholic mother. Her boyfriend committed suicide at age 13. Later, while pursuing the occult, Liesl became a heavy drug user and attempted to commit suicide by slitting her wrists. She was placed in an asylum. After escaping, she entered the black-market drug scene. Twice, she recalls people shouting claims to her that God could do anything, even heal the addicted. Although such "Christian badgering" angered her, Liesl decided to return to the asylum and seek help. A couple of Christian visitors came to her unexpectedly—eventually leading her into a commitment to Jesus as Lord and Savior. Since that time her life has never been the same. She left the world of drugs and suicide and has become committed to helping others.

Mike: Married to an atheist, although he claimed to be a Christian, he had horrendous problems with his marriage—blaming everything on his wife. His anger turned into rage, which he directed at her at even the slightest provocation. At wit's end, he was ready to divorce his wife. He complained to God that, since he was "the Christian," everything was his unbelieving wife's fault and it was of no use to go on. He vowed to get his own life straightened out after the divorce. When he confronted his wife about her unbelief, she first angrily told him, "Quit yelling at me." Unexpectedly, Mike felt inspired to ask her if she believed Jesus was the Son of God. To both their surprise, she said yes, and both chose to receive Jesus as Lord and Savior that evening. Miraculously, their marriage was instantaneously restored.

John: Trapped by sex and drugs and heavily into rock music, John seemed to be on the road to destruction. As his life spiraled downward, his drug use increased, and he found himself financially ruined because of it. By this time, nearly all of his friends were either dead or in jail. Then he started having revelations of all of his past experiences—often bringing him to tears. A friend, recognizing the anguish he was in, suggested he needed to find a relationship with God. Within weeks, John discovered Jesus Christ and God's saving grace. Upon accepting Jesus as Lord and Savior, he was set free from his troubled past.

Experiences like these happen every day, and they are evidence of the love that comes into a person's life in a relationship with God.

Prophecies of Crucifixion

Crucifixion, perhaps the most excruciating and horrible execution method ever devised, was not known until 519 B.C., when it was instituted by Darius I, the king of Persia.[30] The Bible, however, prophesied that the Messiah would be "pierced" long before that time—in about 1000 B.C.:

> *A band of evil men has encircled me, they have pierced my hands and my feet.*
>
> —PSALM 22:16

The prophet Zechariah also prophesied that the Messiah would be "pierced":

> *They will look on me, the one they have pierced, and they will mourn for him as one mourns for an only child, and grieve bitterly for him as one grieves for a firstborn son.*
>
> —ZECHARIAH 12:10

In addition, many other details of Jesus' death were given in advance:

❖ the Messiah silent at His trial—prophesied 700 years in advance (Isaiah 53:7)

❖ given gall and vinegar—prophesied 1000 years in advance (Psalm 69:21)

❖ others casting lots for His clothing—prophesied 1000 years in advance (Psalm 22:18)

❖ His bones not broken—prophesied 1000 years in advance (Psalm 34:20)

❖ dying with thieves—prophesied 700 years in advance (Isaiah 53:9)

❖ buried in a rich man's grave—prophesied 700 years in advance (Isaiah 53:9)

How could such accurate prophecies have been given so far before the events?

Jellyfish

The Irukandji jellyfish is only 2 centimeters across, but it can kill a human being with the sting of one of its tentacles.[31] Though it has a skin thinner than fine paper that can be torn very easily, the jellyfish survives while being tossed about by waves powerful enough to sink the greatest ships.

A delicate jellyfish—with killing capacity, and able to survive in the most severe environmental conditions.

How did it come to be?

The Reliability of the Scripture Record

Can the words of the Bible be trusted? Were they accurately recorded, or have they been changed? These are critical questions, if one is to accept the Bible's words.

When we question the reliability of the ancient hand-copied Holy Scripture of the Jews, we often think of it as if we were hand-copying a document in the twenty-first century. Today, we would certainly expect that errors would be made almost every time a document were hand-copied. In today's thinking, we would thus expect a document—several centuries hence—to bear little resemblance to the original.

Practices and Ceremonies

However, there are several fundamental differences between hand-copying a document today versus at the time of Moses. Perhaps most importantly is the state of mind of the Jewish nation, which was a theocracy—a nation governed by God. The holy writings—especially the law of Moses (the first five books of the Bible)—were treated with utmost respect and care. Copies were closely monitored in the copying process and checked thereafter for accuracy. (We must keep in mind that the laws of Moses governed not only religious activities, but also judicial activities.)

The practices and ceremonies surrounding the copying of Holy Scripture demonstrated the importance attached to it. First, scribes trained for years to prepare for this important task. They could not practice their profession until age 30. Second, a ceremonial washing was required prior to the copying of any Scripture. Third, the name of God was also regarded with enormous reverence. The scribes, fearful of using the Lord God's name in vain (the third commandment) would write the name of God with the middle letters missing (that is, *YHWH* was written as *Y_ _H*). So important was the name of God that, whenever it was about to be written, scribes would say a "sanctification prayer."

The holy scrolls were themselves regarded with extreme reverence. At the end of the useful life of the master scrolls, they were actually given a ceremonial burial.

Scriptural Copy Rules

The scribes were required to adhere to very precise rules, along with the discipline that was ingrained in them in their years of training. The many rules that started with the Old Testament scribes and continued with the New Testament copyists included very precise, even extreme, requirements for the preparation of and copying of manuscripts.[32]

Apart from these special requirements were the basic scribal rules. The word scribes literally means "counters." To verify the accuracy of every scroll that was copied, they had several items that were counted. They counted every letter and compared it to the master scroll. They counted the number of words. And as a final crosscheck, they would count through each scroll to the halfway point and compare the letter with the "halfway letter" of the master scroll.

Hence, the precision of the Old Testament scribes and the New Testament "professional" copyists was enormous—far different from what one might expect today.

Memorization of Scripture Increases Reliability

Imagine attempting to alter history by altering the words of Holy Scripture. Succeeding would require changing a high percentage of all written Scripture to ensure that contradictions didn't exist.

However, if someone really wanted to change Holy Scripture, changing all the written scrolls would still not be enough. Virtually all of the Jews memorized vast amounts of Scripture. It was a vital part of their education. Hence, if someone had wanted to change Scripture for some reason, they would not only have to have changed the many copies, but would have had to change the memories of the Jewish people as well. It would have been impossible.

Knowing that the original manuscripts of the Bible were regarded as important governmental and holy documents and that they were accurately copied from generation to generation provides us assurance that the early biblical manuscripts we possess are accurate. When we combine this information with the plethora of early, consistent manuscripts (see reason 42), we can be virtually certain that today's Bible is an accurate representation of the autographs. Scriptural duplication procedures provide confidence that we possess accurate copies of the original Bible.

Xi: The Remarkable Subatomic Particle

Just when it seems things can't get any smaller or more ephemeral, science finds something new. Enter the amazing *xi* particle, a subatomic particle found in all living things.

Once we thought that protons, electrons, and neutrons were the only particles comprising the atom. Since then we have identified more than 200 additional subatomic particles. However, of all these, the xi has the shortest life span—a mere ten-billionth of a second. So, in only one second, xi particles in a human body have undergone billions of lifetimes. The human body contains some 10^{28} atoms, which—with xi particles coming in and out of existence in less than a billionth of a second—are turning over at a rate of a billion trillion per second.[33] Therefore we can infer that a human body is changing at virtually the speed of light.

The xi particle provides evidence of incredible design at the submicroscopic level. Furthermore, it yields insight into the instantaneous renewal of living things on an ongoing basis, which points to a Renewer and Creator.

Atheism: Impossible to Prove

Anyone claiming to be an atheist implies that there is suffi-cient evidence to prove God doesn't exist. In other words, if someone rejects theism due to insufficient evidence, they imply there is sufficient evidence to accept atheism. Otherwise, their conclusion would be irrational.

However, it is clearly impossible to prove atheism, because this proof would require what philosophers define as a *negative existential*—that is, a statement to the effect that a certain thing does *not* exist. To prove this statement, we would literally have to review every single "thing" and verify that it is not the "thing" (in this case, God) that is being sought. Naturally, this is impossible.

However, in the case of "proving" the existence of God, a more practical approach can be taken. Reasonable "proof"—the kind we commonly accept statistically in the standards of the laws of physics in practical forms—such as in the engineering of bridges—can be applied to show the existence of God.

For example, in the case of origin of life, there are only two alternatives: 1) random chance (evolution being the best-known idea), or 2) special creation (by God). If we can prove that one is impossible, then the other is certain. Origin by random chance can be proven to be impossible (see reason 2).

Likewise, when we evaluate the likelihood of the Bible containing hundreds of perfectly correct prophecies, we find the statistical odds to be beyond reason without God's involvement (see reason 101). Again, this uses a commonly accepted form of statistical "proof" to verify the existence of God—a far better argument than anything an atheist can offer.

Therefore, while it is impossible for an atheist to prove the nonexistence of God, it is not impossible to "prove" the existence of God using the same statistical standards we commonly accept in the building of bridges.

Lightning

A lightning bolt takes only about a half of a second to send a billion volts of electricity through the air. During that time, it heats the air around it to a temperature five times greater than the surface of the sun.[34] The rapidly expanding air around the bolt creates vibration and thunder.

Scientists understand the mechanics of lightning—most typically, negative charges in the clouds attract positive charges in the ground when the two charges get close enough and strong enough—similar to static electricity.

Every second of every day, there are about 100 lightning strikes worldwide. Every year, about 80 people die in the United States from being struck by lightning. However, lightning plays several important, vital roles for life on earth.

First, *lightning "fixes" nitrogen*, creating a natural fertilizer. This has been important through the millennia in promoting the vegetation growth necessary for the production of oxygen for living animals.

Second, *lightning lights forest fires*—about 10,000 per year. While this seems like a harmful effect, in the grand scheme of things it's not. Periodic burning and replenishment of forests is actually healthy for the environment.

Third, *lightning may have been the first source of fire for human beings,* critical for the development of the human race.

What is the source of such an indispensable phenomenon?

The Septuagint

It didn't take long after the conquest of the Middle East by Alexander the Great in 331 B.C. until most of the Jewish people outside of Palestine gave up their native language of Hebrew in favor of Greek. When this happened, only scribes and a select group of other educated people had the capability to read Holy Scripture. Recognizing this problem, the Jews of Egypt appointed a group of 70 scholars (hence the name *Septuagint*, meaning "seventy") to translate the Old Testament into Greek. This happened around 250 B.C.

The Septuagint was the Scripture in common usage at the time of Jesus. In fact, most of the quotations of the Old Testament (Hebrew Scriptures) in the New Testament are from the Septuagint. It would have been the Scripture that Jesus used to minister to the common person. In fact, Christians adopted the Septuagint so wholeheartedly that the Jews ultimately lost interest in it and regarded it to be the "Christian Old Testament." Even today, it is regarded as the official Old Testament version by the Greek Orthodox Church.

Today we have fragments of the Septuagint that date back to before 200 B.C. Some fragments of the Septuagint were found among the Dead Sea scrolls (the majority of the scrolls were in Hebrew).

There are several reasons why the Septuagint translation is especially important:

❖ As mentioned, it was the Old Testament version used by Jesus and therefore commands special consideration.

❖ Like the Dead Sea scrolls, the Septuagint establishes the prophecies about Jesus at a point in time predating Jesus. Therefore we can be certain that the prophecies are not contrived.

❖ The Septuagint was translated from Hebrew Scripture as old as, or slightly older than, the earliest existing Hebrew Scripture we have today (that is, the Dead Sea scrolls). Therefore, it is useful for clarifying any points of contention.

To sum up, the very first approved major translation of the Hebrew Scriptures by the Jews provides important evidence of the reliability of the Bible.

66

The Human Heart

Human engineers can't comprehend it. The heart is an amazing machine that beats 100,000 times a day, or about two-and-a-half billion times in a lifetime. In an average life span, about 60 million gallons of blood are pumped.

The most remarkable thing is that the heart does not take a rest during that entire period. There is no time for maintenance. If the heart has a problem, in many cases it repairs itself "on the job" by replacing damaged cells with new ones.

Some think that this incredible machine came about by evolutionary random chance. How could random chance have put all the pieces together at once in such a fortuitous and effective way? How would it "know" what to do?

Engineers, when they compare the heart to man-made pumps, marvel at its design, effectiveness, and efficiency. To many, it is obviously a design by a "master engineer."

Jesus' Entry into Jerusalem: Precisely Forecast

Perhaps the most amazing prophecy in the Bible is the prophecy of the exact day on which Jesus allowed Himself to be called king—His entry into Jerusalem just a few days before His crucifixion (commonly called Palm Sunday). The prophet Daniel was in the midst of praying, when the angel Gabriel came to him with this announcement:

> Seventy "sevens" are decreed for your people and your holy city to finish transgression, to put an end to sin, to atone for wickedness, to bring in everlasting righteousness, to seal up vision and prophecy and to anoint the most holy.
>
> Know and understand this: From the issuing of the decree to restore and rebuild Jerusalem until the Anointed One, the ruler, comes, there will be seven "sevens," and sixty-two "sevens." It will be rebuilt with streets and a trench, but in times of trouble. After the sixty-two "sevens," the Anointed One will be cut off and will have nothing. The people of the ruler who will come will destroy the city and the

> sanctuary. The end will come like a flood: War will
> continue until the end, and desolations have been
> decreed. He will confirm a covenant with many for
> one "seven." In the middle of the "seven" he will put
> an end to sacrifice and offering. And on a wing [of
> the temple] he will set up an abomination that causes
> desolation, until the end that is decreed is poured out
> on him.
>
> —DANIEL 9:24-27

Some essential points in this prophecy are:

1. The first seven "sevens," or 49 years, is the length of time
    for something (perhaps completion of the restoration and
    rebuilding of Jerusalem?).

2. A total of 69 periods of "seven" (that is, 7 + 62) will pass
    from the decree to rebuild Jerusalem until the coming of
    the "Anointed One" (*Messiah*, in Hebrew). This dates to
    the time of Jesus' entry into Jerusalem on Palm Sunday.

3. After that, the Anointed One will be cut off (Hebrew *yikaret*,
    meaning a sudden, violent end—such as crucifixion).

The "periods of seven" could be expressed in days or years.
Other evidence suggests that this prophecy is based on "sevens"
of years. The starting point for this prophecy is the decree by the
Persian king Artaxerxes to rebuild Jerusalem, given on March 5,
444 B.C. (on the first day of the month of Nisan that year—see
Nehemiah 2:1-6).

"Seven Sevens"

We find two interesting historical facts regarding the "seven
sevens," or 49 years, indicated in the prophecy (verse 25): 1) It

took 49 years to restore Jerusalem; and 2) Forty-nine years after 444 B.C., the Old Testament canon was completed (with the book of Malachi).

"Sixty-Nine Sevens"

Adding the "seven sevens" to the sixty-two "sevens," we come up with 69 "sevens," or 483 years. Using the standard Jewish year of 360 days, we arrive at a total of 173,880 days from the day of the decree until the arrival of the Anointed One. The question becomes, does this number of days correspond to the day that Jesus entered Jerusalem on a donkey (Palm Sunday)?

The difference between 444 B.C. and A.D. 33 is 476 solar years (note: there is no year zero). We know there are 365 days, 5 hours, 48 minutes, and 45.975 seconds in a solar year. Multiplying 476 solar years by 365.242198 days, we come to 173,855 days. Hence there is a difference of 25 days between Daniel's prophecy and the actual solar years from 444 B.C. and A.D. 33.

To coordinate the two, it is necessary to take the starting point of March 5 and add 25 days to arrive at the actual date specified by the prophecy. Adding these brings the prophecy date to March 30, A.D. 33, which is the tenth of Nisan in the Jewish Calendar— the date of Palm Sunday (the triumphal entry) that year.

The Passover lamb was selected on the tenth of Nisan, which would have been the day that Jesus entered Jerusalem as the ultimate Passover lamb prior to His crucifixion. Hence, the prophecy precisely predicts the day Jesus entered Jerusalem allowing Himself to be called king! And as prophesied, He was "cut off" after His entry as the Anointed One—by His crucifixion.

How could this remarkable prophecy occur by coincidence?

Michelangelo

Consider the grace and tenderness of Mary holding Jesus in the *Pietá*.

Consider the majesty in God's eyes as He reaches His hand out lovingly to Adam, as depicted on the ceiling of the Sistine Chapel.

Where did Michelangelo get his gift?

The Gaia Phenomenon: The Earth's Self-Regulation of Temperature and Oxygen

Scientists now have concluded that the Earth's self-regulation of temperature and oxygen levels is no accident. Both critical parameters appear to have been designed so that they could be maintained within the narrow range required for life over long periods of time.

Some scientists, such as James Lovelock, believe that oxygen levels should have fluctuated greatly over recent ages.[35] Others estimate that fluctuations in either direction would spell disaster: More than a 25-percent level of oxygen would result in runaway spontaneous fires, and a level below 15 percent would suffocate many higher life forms. Yet the oxygen level has mysteriously remained at about 21 percent ever since mammals have been around. How? Why?

Likewise, the temperature level of planet Earth is surprisingly consistent. This is dependent on many factors, including 1) the absorption of heat by the earth; 2) the ratio of water to land, with a greater amount of land in the Northern Hemisphere, which helps create ocean currents; 3) the protective qualities of the atmosphere; 4) the movement of the ocean currents and atmosphere currents; and 5) the evaporation of water. The number of differing temperate zones, along with the relatively narrow range of temperature fluctuation in each, allows for an unusually large number of life forms on Earth.

While we understand something about the mechanism for oxygen and temperature change, we don't know how it regulates itself. In other words, we don't understand the "thermostat." How are the earth's oxygen level and temperature so precisely maintained over long periods of time—so that they're perfect for human beings?

Archaeological Evidence for the Site of Jesus' Ascension

Jesus' last act on Earth was His ascension into heaven (Luke 24:50-53; Acts 1:9). The place of this event was noted by early Christian writers (for example, Aetheria in the year 381), but no mention of a church was made. A Church of the Ascension was apparently founded by Helena, the mother of the Emperor Constantine, and its existence was noted by the pilgrim Egeria late in the fourth century. It was further verified as existing by about the year 404, when it was described by Jerome. Destroyed by the Persians in 614, it was rebuilt by the year 670, when Arculf speaks of the "last footprints" of the Lord being visible by the light of an "eternally" burning lamp. In 1187, the church was taken over by the Muslims and turned into a mosque, which it remains today.

A "step" in the rock where Jesus is said to have ascended has been preserved inside the building (Jesus is one of the great prophets of Islam).[36]

The archaeological evidence of the site of the ascension of Jesus does not prove that it happened, but it does prove that early Christians *believed* that Jesus existed and ascended into heaven as the Bible indicated. Archaeological identification of the site supports the account contained in the Bible.

The Stars Are Uncountable

At one time it was thought there were about 1100 stars in the universe. In about A.D. 100, Ptolemy was actively cataloging and naming stars—certainly at that time the leading scholars thought the stars were countable.

Yet the prophet Jeremiah described the stars as "uncountable" in about 600 B.C. (Jeremiah 33:22).

Astronomers now estimate there about 100 billion stars in our galaxy and further estimate there are about 100 billion galaxies. If someone started counting stars at a rate of 10 per second (try it—that is impossibly fast), it would take more than 100 trillion years to count all the stars—obviously impossible.

Over and over, science has proven the Bible was right all along, which indicates that God inspired the Bible.

We Can Talk

Studies have shown that animals can communicate in varying degrees through the noises they make. Different types of grunts may relate to the different types of predators threatening them, or they may be specific to courting or mating. On the other hand, there is no evidence of communication in the animal world that comes anywhere close to rivaling the communication human beings achieve through speech.

Consider the precision with which we talk. Engineers can describe electronic components with such exactness that one person can duplicate a complicated part from a discussion on the phone. Poets can pen words that make people laugh, or cry, or experience any of an immense range of emotions. Mothers can express words of deep love to their young.

How did human beings obtain the gift of language?

The Prophecy of Jesus' Birth in Bethlehem

Among the many cities of the world, Bethlehem is tiny. It was even tiny in Jesus' day—estimated to have a population of between 2000 and 4000. It was so small, it wasn't even mentioned when Joshua listed the important cities of Judah (Joshua 15:48-60). Yet the Bible accurately prophesied that Jesus would be born there.

> *But you, Bethlehem Ephrathah,*
> *though you are small among the clans of Judah,*
> *out of you will come for me*
> *one who will be ruler over Israel,*
> *whose origins are from of old,*
> *from ancient times.*
> —Micah 5:2

The Bible clearly associates this prophecy with Jesus (Matthew 2:3-6). Jesus is further identified as being existent at the beginning of creation (John 1), hence fulfilling the prophecy that the "ruler" would have "origins...from of old, from ancient times."

Also interesting is that the correct Bethlehem is identified—the Bethlehem in Ephrathah (Ephrathah would be like one of today's counties). There was another Bethlehem closer to Joseph and Mary's home in Nazareth.

The odds of such a small city being coincidentally selected in a prophecy are extremely small…without divine inspiration.

Black Holes

Einstein's general relativity theory (now essentially a law of physics) predicts the existence of black holes—an astounding cosmological phenomenon.

To understand what a black hole is, it is easiest to first think of it in terms of escape velocity of a gravitational field. For example, earth has a certain gravitational force. It is necessary for a spaceship, for example, to reach a speed of 25,000 miles per hour to escape the pull of gravity of earth (called *escape velocity*).

In some cases, a celestial body (such as a neutron star) is massive enough that the tightly packed neutrons collapse under their own gravity. In such a case, the star would reach a point of "zero" volume, and the curvature of space–time surrounding it would become infinite. The result is that the escape velocity at that point is greater than the speed of light—even light itself cannot escape (hence the term "black hole").

There is substantial evidence that black holes actually do exist—Cygnus X-1 is the designation given to one. Even noted physicists who once rejected black holes (such as astrophysicist Stephen Hawking) now concede they exist.

Since general relativity indicates that both time and space (the universe, that is) are finite, and the existence of black holes points to the evidence that the curvature of space–time surrounding them is infinite, all this suggests that something outside of time and space must exist and must have created them.

Hostile Witnesses

Hostile *witnesses* have long been regarded in courts of law to be among the most compelling of witnesses—because when they make any significant points supporting the claim of a side they are opposed to (or were opposed to), they are very credible. There are several very well-known, important, and credible ancient hostile witnesses to the life of Jesus.

Saul of Tarsus (later Paul) was the leading persecutor of Christians in the years immediately following Jesus' crucifixion (Acts 7:57–8:3). He played an important role at the stoning of Stephen, the first recorded Christian martyr. When Paul took his attack to Damascus, he saw the risen Christ—who spoke to him. His life was never the same.

Paul was transformed overnight from one of the most ardent persecutors of Christians to, perhaps, the greatest evangelist for Jesus of all time. He started more early churches than any other leader and wrote more books of the New Testament than anyone else. Why did Paul give up a life of wealth, power, and prestige, for a life of poverty, persecution, and eventual martyrdom? He had become thoroughly convinced that Jesus rose from the dead, was God incarnate, and promised heavenly rewards.

The brothers of Jesus—*James and Jude*—at first rejected Jesus as God incarnate. Perhaps since they had grown up with Him, Jesus seemed like any other human being. Later, however, they too became believers and apostles. James became the leader of the Christian church in Jerusalem, and each brother wrote a book of the New Testament.

Constantine was the emperor of Rome during the height of Christian persecution, when he saw a vision of the risen Christ. Shortly thereafter, he had a dream that he should go into battle under a banner signifying a belief in the risen Christ. After consulting with Christian leaders, he decided to follow the instructions he believed Jesus had given him. The famous historian, Eusebius—a close associate of Constantine—wrote about these incidents and claims that Constantine swore under oath to their truthfulness.

Constantine's acceptance of Christianity eventually led to the end of persecution (in the year 313) and paved the way for Christianity's growth into the largest religion in the world. It would have been easier—and more "politically correct"—for Constantine to maintain the status quo. Instead, he chose Jesus—a decision that forced him into war with others who opposed his religious view.

All of these originally hostile witnesses took a risk. They all gave up security that could have been maintained by rejecting, or remaining indifferent to, Jesus. Yet all gave up that security for one reason—the belief that Jesus was who He claimed to be.

Pacific Anchovies

L ike thousands of shiny, silver ornaments, they travel quickly through the water of the Pacific Ocean. Suddenly, without warning, as if on cue, they dart—all at once—to their left. Moments later, as if orchestrated, they dart back to their right. Thousands upon thousands, all at precisely the same second.

How did the tiny Pacific anchovies come to be? How can they possibly know how to dart to and fro at precisely the same time? Who designed such finely tuned, precision controls that work so flawlessly?

The Soul

What defines an individual? Some say appearance. But what happens when appearance changes? When someone gains weight, grows a beard, or gets burned beyond recognition, is he or she any less recognizable—after a few moments of communication?

Taking it a step further, do sounds, movements, or other characteristics define an individual? Again, a person could undergo many changes that mask any or all of these characteristics—perhaps beyond recognition—yet the person would still be the same person. Why?

A person is defined by the soul—that which encompasses one's thoughts, personality, and relationships with people and with God. Only within the soul is the real person known. Consider that even though all the atoms in a person's body are replaced every five years (see reason 32), that person still remembers things from the past, has the same traits, and is the same being.

When life is instilled into a human being, something more than just the mechanical instructions for physical development is granted. That "something" is a person's soul. And the provider of it must be God.

Archaeologist
William Albright

William Foxwell Albright (1891–1971) is known as one of the greatest biblical archaeologists of all time, with more than 800 books and articles, mostly on the validity of biblical manuscripts, to his credit.

Albright is well known for his authentication of the Dead Sea scrolls. Since these scrolls ensure that the Old Testament prophecies were written before the time of Jesus, we can be certain that those prophecies were not contrived after the fact.

Albright also researched and confirmed the dating of the writings of the New Testament. His conclusion was that there is "no longer any solid basis for dating any book of the New Testament after about A.D. 80."[37]

Early in his professional life, Albright had some doubts about the validity of biblical claims about Jesus. Following years of research, he concluded that the Bible was authentic and the claims of Jesus could be trusted—all of which provides additional support for the Bible.

One Second of Sight

In one second of sight, the human optical system—the eye, the optic nerve, and the brain, perform a quantity of computation that would require 100 years of nonstop computer time on the Cray Supercomputer (one of the largest, most advanced computers in the world).[38]

How did this intricate system come to be?

Prophecies of Jesus

The Bible indicates that prophecy originates from God:

> *I make known the end from the beginning, from*
> *ancient times, what is still to come.*
>
> —ISAIAH 46:10

Jesus indicated that He is God (for example, in John 10:30: "I and the Father are one"). He declared that there is no other ("No one comes to the Father except through me"—John 14:6). Jesus prophesied many things, most significantly His own resurrection—three times:

> *From that time on Jesus began to explain to his dis-*
> *ciples that he must go to Jerusalem and suffer many*
> *things at the hands of the elders, chief priests and*
> *teachers of the law, and that he must be killed and on*
> *the third day be raised to life.*
>
> —MATTHEW 16:21

When they came together in Galilee, he said to them, "The Son of Man is going to be betrayed into the hands of men. They will kill him, and on the third day he will be raised to life."
—MATTHEW 17:22-23

"We are going up to Jerusalem, and the Son of Man will be betrayed to the chief priests and the teachers of the law. They will condemn him to death and will turn him over to the Gentiles to be mocked and flogged and crucified. On the third day he will be raised to life!"
—MATTHEW 20:18-19

Other prophecies of Jesus include the following:

❖ One of His disciples would betray Him (Matthew 26:21; Mark 14:17-21; Luke 22:21-22).

❖ He did not come to abolish the Law but to fulfill it prophetically (Matthew 5:17-20).

❖ His disciples would desert Him on the night of the Passover feast (Matthew 26:30-31; Mark 14:26-27).

❖ Peter would disown Him three times (Matthew 26:33-34; Mark 14:29-30; Luke 22:31-34).

❖ He would be crucified (John 3:14-16).

❖ He would be "lifted up"—that is, hung on a cross (John 12:32-34).

❖ He would be resurrected (Matthew 26:32-34; Mark 14:28-31; John 2:19).

❖ There would be a "miraculous sign" "like Jonah"—His resurrection after three days and three nights (Matthew 12:39-41; 16:4; Luke 11:29-32).

❖ If His body were destroyed, He would raise it in three days (John 2:19).

❖ Jerusalem would be destroyed (Luke 19:42-44).

Jesus Himself testified to His own deity. He then prophesied many miraculous things that would verify it—the most spectacular being His death and resurrection after three days. The fulfillment of all of these prophecies provides evidence that Jesus was who He said He was.

Hope

Christianity offers hope. It offers hope for a good life on earth and for eternal life in paradise. Most importantly, this hope is not based on "earning it" or "doing good." Instead it's based on God's grace, and God's grace alone.

> *It is by grace you have been saved, through faith—*
> *and this not from yourselves, it is the gift of God—*
> *not by works, so that no one can boast.*
> —EPHESIANS 2:8-10

Some say Christianity is too narrow since it states that the only way to be reconciled with God is through accepting Jesus Christ, making Him Lord and Savior. Such people may feel that God is too big to be accessed by Jesus alone, and that God must therefore be part of many religions.

However, the issue isn't what people *think*—it's what is *true*. What is testable regarding the truth? The evidence for Jesus—His sacrifice by crucifixion and His resurrection—is overwhelming. Likewise, the evidence for the Bible and the God of the Bible is overwhelming. With this knowledge, a wise person would listen to this invitation and also heed the warning:

*God so loved the world that he gave his one and only
Son, that whoever believes in him shall not perish
but have eternal life. For God did not send his Son
into the world to condemn the world, but to save the
world through him. Whoever believes in him is not
condemned, but whoever does not believe stands condemned already because he has not believed in the
name of God's one and only Son.*

—JOHN 3:16-18

In the above verses, the Greek word "believe" has a fuller
meaning than in contemporary English. It implies an actual *acceptance* of Jesus. One thing to note from the above verses, especially
John 3:16, is the incredible element of love from God. He permitted Jesus, who is God Himself (part of the Trinity), to endure
the most painful, humiliating death known in order to provide
salvation to anyone accepting Him. Not accepting this free gift is
like a "slap in the face" to God. How could anyone not believe that
Jesus' blood is "good enough"?

Imagine a person jumping in front of a speeding truck and
dying to save your child or most cherished friend. Could you
imagine *not* being forever indebted to that person? *Jesus* is that
person—available to anyone. Of course we are indebted to Him.

So the question becomes, why not accept Jesus as Lord and
Savior? Evidence of His existence and sacrifice is abundant. Even
if some doubt exists, doesn't it make sense to accept Him based
on the knowledge available anyway? After all, it's simple, it's free,
and there is nothing to lose.

The Bible promises hope and eternal life through grace richly
provided by God in His gift—the gift of Jesus.

The Site of the Last Supper

The meal on the night before Jesus was crucified is believed to have taken place in the house belonging to His follower John Mark's mother. Other events said to have taken place there include

- ❖ Jesus' washing the disciples' feet

- ❖ the meeting of the disciples after the resurrection (Luke 24:33-49)

- ❖ the receiving of the Holy Spirit by the disciples at Pentecost (Acts 2:1-4)

- ❖ the death of Jesus' mother, Mary

Early Christians identified the site and many writers later confirmed it, including Origen (about the year 250), Eusebius (in 300), Aetheria (in 381), Jerome (in 400), and Theodosius (in 530).

A "great church" was built on the site—located on Mount Zion only 200 "paces" from Golgotha (the site of the crucifixion of Jesus). The church was destroyed by the Persians in 614 and later rebuilt.

Excavations in and around the church have located part of a first-century "synagogue" that seems to be similar to the "house–synagogue" created in the house of Peter after the resurrection (see reason 21). It may have been built in the house of John Mark's mother. Interestingly, a niche that was used to hold Holy Scripture was oriented toward Golgotha instead of in the customary direction towards the Temple. This probably reflected a change in worship based on Jesus' once-for-all sacrifice.

The identification of this site by early Christians indicates early belief in the events that occurred there. It helps confirm the historical accuracy of the Bible.

Free Will

Pierre-Simon de Laplace (1749–1827) is typical of philoso-phers who embraced determinism: the concept that all actions were based on a predetermined cause. The implication was that everything in the future was predictable and predeter-mined. While the laws of physics seem to back this up (for example, dropping a ball will always have the same result), it is harder to apply the same logic to choices of people. Nonetheless, philosophers did so—explaining that every "fork-in-a-road" choice is made based on a chain of preceding events that make the choice predictable.

The Bible indicates that human beings have free will despite the fact that God already knows the beginning from the end (Isaiah 46:9-10), implying predetermination. How are both pos-sible? Is there any scientific explanation for what appears to be an impossible biblical paradox?

Einstein's theory of general relativity, now verified as thor-oughly as other laws of physics, provides an explanation for how there can be free will—despite seeming predetermination by an all-knowing God.

Essentially, general relativity indicates that time—and any action within time—is relative to the speed at which something is traveling. Furthermore, if something were traveling at the speed of light, time would virtually stand still. Thus, if God is light (as the Bible indicates—1 John 1:5) and God is infinite, then time would stand still for God for the past, the present, and the future. To God, everything would be seen and would be predetermined. To anyone traveling within that "slower-than-light" time domain, there would be free-will choice. Hence, science supports the paradox of the existence of free will in a world of determinism, so to speak, as indicated in the Bible.

Fire

Fire has been vital to the survival and growth of humanity. There is no period of human existence in whose artwork fire was not present.

Interestingly, fire has been used in religious ceremonies of all kinds through the millennia. The Bible speaks of fire in many places. It was used to judge Sodom and Gomorrah (Genesis 19:24), yet it was also used to demonstrate the glory of God (Exodus 13:21; 24:17). Fire was an integral part of the sacrifice commanded by God (Exodus 12:8; 29:18).

Was it just a coincidence that man discovered and harnessed fire?

The Cave of Jesus' End-Time Revelation

Jesus gave His so-called Olivet Discourse (Matthew 24:3–25:46) on the Mount of Olives towards the end of His ministry. In this revelation to His disciples, Jesus reviews in some detail the events leading up to and occurring at the end of time.

Certainly this would have been a memorable event for the disciples, and presumably one that they told others about later. Therefore, it would be natural for early Christians to remember and later venerate the site where this occurred. In fact they did.

Eusebius, writing in the early 300s, tells of a church that was erected to honor the cave where Jesus gave these revelations. Excavation has located this church, which was built by Helena, the emperor Constantine's mother. Other witnesses to this include 1) the Bordeaux Pilgrim, who upon seeing the church in the year 333, said it was located at the place "where before the Passion, the Lord taught the disciples"; 2) Aetheria (active 381–384), who indicated that "the cave in which the Lord used to teach is there"; and 3) Nicephorus (829) tells of climbing marble stairs built to lead up to the church built by Helena.

The authentication of the place where Jesus instructed the disciples helps verify the account in the Bible.

Mental Organization

It is easy to take for granted the miracle of how our mind works. Yet, when we think about it, it's really quite amazing how initial thoughts become actionable ideas.

First, there is the issue of *imagination*. How do thoughts originate in and of themselves? Often there is no basis for a thought—it just seems to occur. What causes creativity or abstract thinking?

Second, there is the issue of *order*. For a thought to be of value, it has to be related to something—in order to cause an emotion, result in an action, or lead to additional thoughts that bring a final result. The process of ordering thoughts is hierarchal. (It would seem that a randomly developed situation would be chaotic—the state of greatest entropy—or at a minimum, non-hierarchal.)

Third, there is the issue of *evaluation*. How is it that we can judge the relative merits (or right or wrong) of thoughts or ideas? Why is it that we simply know that certain things are pleasing, such as harmonious chords or beautiful patterns and color combinations, while others are displeasing?

Think about the writing of this "reason 86." First the idea had to be conceived. Then it had to be ordered in a way that made sense. And now your mind is evaluating it to see if it makes a good point. Nothing in the material world leads to such mental organization…yet human beings have this ability. Why?

The Existence of the
Christian Church

Nobody doubts the existence of the Christian church. Not only is Christianity the largest religion in the world, but it has survived persecution ever since its founding—shortly after the crucifixion of Jesus in about A.D. 33. It exists in every corner of the world, even where it is strictly prohibited under the threat of death.

In the year 33, the Jewish population is estimated to have been less than one half of one percent of that of the world—and virtually all early Christians came from among the Jews. However, while the Jewish population as a percentage of the world population remains about the same today, the number of Christians has exploded and now represents about one-third of the world's population.

The foundation of the Christian church is the resurrection of Jesus Christ. This, as prophesied by Jesus Himself, indicates that He was truly divine. It is an extremely powerful historical premise. The Christian church is not a philosophical religion like Hinduism, Buddhism, or various New Age religions. Instead, Christianity is tied to one central historical issue—*that the resurrection of Jesus Christ is historical fact.*

Christianity can be evaluated and confirmed by that single historical event. If it occurred, then Jesus in fact is Lord and Savior. If not, He is not.

When considering the existence of the church in light of the conditions at the time, we should not only consider the miracle of the resurrection itself, but also the church surviving in spite of massive persecution, and the theological difficulty of accepting the idea of the Trinity, in which Jesus is God. (The idea of a triune God required a fundamental change in thinking for the highly monotheistic Jews.)

The existence of the church shows that millions of people have overcome all three of these difficulties and believed in the historical resurrection. Backed up by lives of martyrs who died for the historical fact of the resurrection, the church provides strong evidence supporting the existence of God, the deity of Jesus, and the truth of the Bible.

Earth: The Only Perfect Place for Life

In recent years, scientists have started listing the various parameters necessary to support life on planet Earth. In addition, they have estimated the likelihood of finding such life-specific factors on another planet. The results were surprising. And the number of parameters discovered has rapidly increased—now more than 150 life-specific requirements have been defined.[39]

Some parameters are obvious, such as the distance from the earth to the sun. We know that if the earth were closer, our environment would be too hot. If further away, it would be too cold. Scientists estimate that the probability that another planet would fall within the acceptable range of distance from its star (in our case, the sun) is about 1 chance in 1000. Other life-support factors are not so obvious, such as the size of the star's galaxy, the age of the star, the planet's number of moons, the tilt of the axis of the planet, the thickness of the planet's crust, the amount of cobalt in the crust—the list goes on and on.

The probability of all these necessary requirement items existing in a planet is 1 chance in 10^{166}. However, scientists estimate that the maximum possible number of planets in the universe is only about 10^{22}. Taking the number of planets and dividing it by the odds ($10^{22}/10^{166}$) provides the odds that any one planet in the universe would have all of the necessary life-support parameters. The odds are only 1 chance in 10^{144}. This is virtually zero. The evidence suggests that Earth is the only planet where life exists, and that it was planned by a Master Designer.

The Jewish Exile
to Babylon

Imagine someone telling you that all the people of the United States would be exiled to Brazil, and that Washington, D.C.—in particular, the Capitol—would be razed. Imagine further that the length of the exile would be exactly 90 years, after which time a man named Egbert would allow the people to return to the United States and to rebuild Washington and the Capitol. Sound far-fetched? Of course.

The people of Israel were told the same thing in about 700 B.C. Only replace the United States with Israel; Brazil with Babylon; the Capitol with the Temple; 90 years with 70 years; and Egbert with Cyrus. Now take it one step further—absolutely everything came true exactly as predicted by Isaiah and other prophets in the Bible!

The prophecies were made more than 100 years before the exile—more than 100 years before Cyrus, the Medo-Persian king, was even born! Evidence of their fulfillment is given not only by various writings, but also by archaeology. A commemorative stone called the *Cyrus Cylinder* was discovered, which recorded Cyrus's proclamation allowing the Jews to return to Jerusalem to rebuild the city and the Temple.

The odds of the chance fulfillment of all of the prophecies of the Jewish exile to Babylon without a single mistake are beyond reason. How did the prophets of the Bible know such precise events in advance?

Morality

From early childhood, all people sense certain objective moral laws that govern right and wrong. This does not mean that people always choose to follow the path of righteousness—simply that they know it. For example, they know that it is inherently wrong to murder, steal, rape, and lie.

The existence of such a moral law implies the existence of a moral Lawgiver. Moral laws don't describe what is, but are instead an indication of what ought to be. A moral lawgiver would be the source of the built-in morality that all human beings possess.

The moral Lawgiver would, of necessity, be supreme. His discernment would have to be perfect. The only way to describe such a perfect, supreme moral Lawgiver would be *God*.

Four Hundred Years
of History Predicted

In about 538 B.C., the prophet Daniel predicted nearly 400 years of history, as recorded by his scribes in Daniel chapter 8 of the Bible. His prophecy started with a prediction that the Babylonians would be overthrown by the Medians and the Persians, after which the ruler of Persia (Cyrus) would allow the Jews to return from exile. This would be followed by a very rapid conquest by Greece—which at the time of the prophecy was a relatively weak nation. This prophecy came true with the rise of Alexander the Great, who conquered the region with incredible speed.

Greece was represented in the prophecy as a goat with a large horn that "broke off" at the height of its power and was replaced by four smaller horns. In fact, Alexander the Great (the large horn) suddenly died at the height of his power and was succeeded by four other leaders of lesser power.

Following the reign by the "four horns," another small horn "grew out of one of them" and grew in power to the south and to the east. In history, this "horn" represented Antiochus IV Epiphanes, who in the second century was the ruler of the Seleucid empire. The prophecy goes on to state that the empire would grow towards the "Beautiful Land" (Israel) and that it would set itself up as the "Prince of the host"—taking away daily sacrifice and "throwing truth to the ground." In history, that's exactly what Antiochus IV Epiphanes did. Worship and sacrifice at the Temple was stopped, and an abomination—the sacrifice of a pig (detestable to the Jews) on the Temple altar was committed.

The accuracy of this prophecy of 400 years of history is beyond coincidence. It confirms that God inspired the Bible.

The Journey of the
Red Blood Cell

The cell bangs from side to side in its rapid pass through the left ventricle of the heart. Then it slips into the artery leading to the left arm.

Every beat of the heart pushes the cell farther along its journey. It passes from large arteries to smaller veins. Finally it squeezes into the tiniest of capillaries and releases its cargo of oxygen and nutrition into the cells awaiting its arrival. All of this occurs within a matter of seconds.

How does the red blood cell "know" what to do? How does it "know" where to go? How does it "know" what cells need oxygen?

After traveling about through myriad passages of arteries, veins, and capillaries, the cell returns to the heart within 60 seconds, only to turn around and take the same journey again to a different body part. Around and around the cell travels, touring every inch of the body over its life of 120 days—an incredible adventure. On about the 200,001st trip, the red blood cell reaches its final destination, the spleen, where it is recycled.[40] It has served its purpose—and another red blood cell has already been created to take its place.

Is the red blood cell simply a result of random physical development? In a newly conceived fetus, an immature "heart" first appears about 3 weeks after conception. By 14 weeks, it is already pumping 7 gallons per day (an adult heart pumps about 2000 gallons per day). A complex network of arteries, veins, and capillaries expands within the rapidly growing fetus. These vessels are so intricately and precisely designed that every single cell is accounted for in its everyday needs for oxygen, nutrition, and waste removal.

Does all of this still seem like a series of random events? Or is it more likely the handiwork of a Creator with design ability far beyond the human imagination?

The Prophecy of Jesus' Ancestors

The Old Testament prophesies the Messiah's ancestors, giving descriptions that precisely fit Jesus' ancestors.

❖ *Abraham:* "Your descendants will take possession of the cities of their enemies, and through your offspring all nations on earth will be blessed, because you have obeyed me" (Genesis 22:17-18).

- *Fulfillment:* "The promises were spoken to Abraham and to his seed. The Scripture does not say 'and to seeds,' meaning many people, but 'and to your seed,' meaning one person, who is Christ" (Galatians 3:16).

❖ *Isaac:* "It is through Isaac that your offspring will be reckoned" (Genesis 21:12).

- *Fulfillment:* "He was...the son of Isaac" (Luke 3:23,34).

❖ *Jacob:* "I see him, but not now; I behold him, but not near. A star will come out of Jacob; a scepter will rise out of Israel" (Numbers 24:17).

- • *Fulfillment:* "He was…the son of Jacob" (Luke 3:23,34).

❖ *Judah:* "The scepter will not depart from Judah, nor the ruler's staff from between his feet, until he comes to whom it belongs and the obedience of the nations is his" (Genesis 49:10).

- • Fulfillment: "He was…the son of Judah" (Luke 3:23,33).

❖ *Jesse:* "A shoot will come up from the stump of Jesse; from his roots a Branch will bear fruit. The Spirit of the LORD will rest on him" (Isaiah 11:1-2).

- • *Fulfillment:* "He was…the son of Jesse," (Luke 3:23,32).

❖ *David:* " 'The days are coming,' declares the LORD, 'when I will raise up to David a righteous Branch, a King who will reign wisely and do what is just and right in the land' " (Jeremiah 23:5).

- • Fulfillment: "He was…the son of David" (Luke 3:23,31).

What are the odds of all of these prophecies coming true in Jesus by accident? Let's make the following assumptions:

❖ *Abraham:* 1 chance in 150 million (estimated number of males in the world of that time[41])

❖ *Isaac:* 1 chance in 2 (Abraham had two sons while his wife Sarah was alive)

❖ *Jacob:* 1 chance in 2 (Isaac had two sons)

❖ *Judah:* 1 chance in 12 (Jacob had twelve sons)

❖ *Jesse:* 1 chance in 240 (Judah had five sons, Perez had at least two sons, Hezron had three sons, Ram had four sons, Amminadab had at least one son, Nahshon had at least one son, Salmon had at least one son, Boaz had at least one son, Obed had at least two sons—thus, 5 x 2 x 3 x 4 x 1 x 1 x 1 x 1 x 2 = 240)

❖ *David:* 1 chance in 8

Total odds of the random fulfillment of all these prophecies in one man are about *1 in 14 trillion* (150,000,000 x 2 x 2 x 12 x 240 x 8 = 13,824,000,000,000).

Therefore, the odds of all of the prophecies of the Messiah's ancestors coming true in Jesus are virtually zero—without divine intervention.

Logic

Logic might be defined as *the principle of correct reasoning.* Human beings intuitively use logic as a tool to arrive at truth. Aristotle (384–322 B.C.) was the first person known to systematize logic. In its most basic form, this system involves 1) claiming a conclusion and 2) supporting that claim with evidence or reasoning based on facts.

To ensure correct reasoning, the following guidelines can be applied:

❖ All premises supporting the conclusion must be based on facts or other intellectually acceptable support.

❖ All premises must be relevant to one another in a reasonable way.

❖ There must be sufficient evidence to support a conclusion.

❖ The evidence must be clear and not ambiguous.

❖ The evidence must be irrefutable.

What gives human beings the desire and capability to use logic to determine truth?

Natural Selection
and Survival

Charles Darwin introduced the concept of *natural selection* as the mechanism that allowed for evolution. Essentially, changes occurring in a species that were favorable to its existence would be propagated genetically, while unfavorable characteristics would not—sometimes causing a species to eventually die out. In the famous peppered moth example, white moths predominated when bark on trees was light-colored, and dark moths predominated when bark was dark-colored. Natural selection was the primary idea that allowed the theory of evolution to become widely accepted.

Ironically, natural selection is actually evidence for the existence of God. Embedded in the DNA molecule is enormous potential for variation. For example, the human DNA structure is made up of 3.2 billion *base pairs* (the "rungs of the ladder" of the DNA). Each base pair contains coded information that defines who a person is. And base pairs are grouped into virtual limitless possibilities of genes and sequences. Eye color, height, body type, skin color, personality traits, intelligence, and many other things are determined by someone's DNA.

Hence, all species have the ability to adapt to many different environmental conditions over time. Natural selection does indeed provide for the "survival of the fittest" that Darwin spoke of. However, it does not allow one species to change into another (as Darwinian evolution claims). Instead, it provides a marvelous means for the continuation of a species—a phenomenon that points to a Designer.

Prophecies of Tyre

The prophet Ezekiel (active 592–570 B.C.) predicted the fate of perhaps the strongest seaport of that time in the Mediterranean, Tyre (located just north of Israel). His predictions included the following:

1. The Babylonian king Nebuchadnezzar would destroy the mainland portion of the city of Tyre (Ezekiel 26:8).

2. Many nations would attack Tyre (verse 3).

3. Tyre would be made a bare rock (verse 4).

4. Fishermen would spread their nets on that rock (verse 5).

5. The debris from the city would be thrown into the water (verse 12).

6. Tyre would never be rebuilt (verse 14).

7. Tyre would never be "found" again (verse 21).

These prophecies were unlikely for such a powerful city. Yet they were all fulfilled precisely as given. Three years after the prophecy was made, Nebuchadnezzar laid siege to the mainland city of Tyre. Thirteen years after the siege began (it lasted from 585 to 573), the city fell to Babylonian control. However, when the gates of the mainland city were finally broken down, the Babylonians found it nearly deserted. The inhabitants had virtually all fled to the island city of Tyre, located about a half mile off the coast. There they continued to reside for several hundred years. The Babylonians destroyed the mainland city, though, fulfilling prediction #1. Nebuchadnezzar's army was made up of soldiers from many nations, fulfilling prediction #2. (Successive attacks by later nations also fulfill this.)

Alexander the Great later attacked Tyre during his campaigns. He scraped the ruins of the destroyed mainland city into the sea to create a large causeway in order to lay siege to the island city. This fulfilled predictions #3 and #5. The bare rock that remained is still used by fishermen for the spreading of nets, fulfilling prediction #4.

While a city called Tyre exists today, it is not the same as the old city—whose site remains bare rock along the coast. Nor does the prominence of the current city even begin to rival the prominence of the ancient city of Tyre, fulfilling prediction #6.

Finally, though one would hardly think that such a great city would "never be found again," in the sense of being "found" in its previous extravagance and glory, the city has certainly remained "lost" (and shows every sign of continuing in this condition).

All of these prophecies coming true implies that God inspired the Bible.

The Taste of an Orange

You bite into it. Microscopic droplets of juice explode into the air and tickle your nose. Your tongue senses the flavor as the juice reaches every part of your mouth. As you chew, the flavor continues to build and enhance your enjoyment. You smile with pleasure. Who provided this delight?

Christian Martyrs

Many early Christians were in a unique position to know for certain whether or not the story of Jesus was true. Some were eyewitnesses to the events of Jesus' life. Others knew eyewitnesses. Others witnessed the martyrdom of the disciples, apostles, and others and were convinced. Many, many Christians were willing to joyfully give their lives for Christ. As Luke put it, they considered it an honor to be considered worthy of suffering for Jesus (Acts 5:41).

The Roman emperor Nero was the first to encourage persecution of Christians on a mass scale. Nero, who had been blamed for the great fire of Rome, attempted to shift the blame to the Christians. Many unimaginably cruel executions were devised. Some Christians were sewn inside skins of wild animals and torn apart by fierce dogs. It was also recorded that some were dressed in waxed shirts, then impaled on poles, and set afire to provide light for orgies held on Nero's behalf.

As the news spread throughout the Roman Empire, Nero's strategy to break the spirit of the Christians backfired. The spirit of the early Christians was instead strengthened—a sign of their enormous conviction and belief in Christ. Many of the 72 appointed by Jesus (Luke 10:1) were martyred.

Nero was simply the first of a long string of emperors of persecution. Emperor Domitian (ruled 81–96) was the first to issue an order that Christians be brought before a tribunal to be questioned about their faith. If they didn't renounce their faith, they were killed. According to tradition, among those martyred during this time was Paul's dear friend Timothy.

Emperor Trajan (ruled 98–117) continued the practice of forcing Christians to renounce their faith—however, they also had to bow down to his statue and worship him to be set free. Christians continued to choose death.

Trajan was succeeded by Hadrian (ruled 117–138), who was responsible for some 10,000 martyrs. He was especially known for placing crowns of thorns on Christians' heads, crucifying them, and thrusting spears in their sides in a mockery of Jesus' crucifixion. (Ironically, however, this simply reinforced the written accounts of Christ's sufferings.) In one case, a Roman commander was ordered by Hadrian to join in idolatrous sacrifice to celebrate his victories. When the commander refused because of his faith in Christ, Hadrian had him and his family put to death.

The key point regarding Christian martyrdom is that it was for a historical event, not merely a philosophical idea.

Ignatius (died in the year 110) was a courageous church leader who ministered to many Christians in hiding during the persecution. Like many Christians at the time, he welcomed the chance to joyously give his life for Christ. When Ignatius realized that he would soon be executed for spreading the gospel of Christ, he is recorded as saying,

> [As for the lions…] I will entice them devour me quickly…Let come on me fire and cross and conflicts with wild beasts, wrenching of bones,

mangling of limbs...only let me reach Jesus
Christ.[42]

The inevitable came, and Ignatius was captured and rushed to
the Colosseum to be executed. He looked to the heavens and said,

I am the wheat of Christ: I am going to be
ground with the teeth of wild beasts that I may
be found pure bread.[43]

From the testimonies of the early Christian martyrs, we can
trust that they truly believed that Jesus is God.

Currents in the Ocean

Today, virtually all oceanfaring vessels make use of the currents that exist in the ocean. These currents have been thoroughly mapped, and among other things, this knowledge provides greater efficiency and safety during travel.

Matthew Fontaine Maury was the first to map the currents in the sea. It is interesting to note what led him to do this in the first place. He was reading the book of Isaiah in the Bible and came upon this verse:

> *This is what the Lord says—he who made a way through the sea, a path through the mighty waters...*
> —ISAIAH 43:16

Maury, assuming that the Bible was correct, started seeking paths in the sea. He eventually discovered many ocean currents and is now considered the father of oceanography.

100

The Existence of Good

The second law of thermodynamics speaks of a universe that is moving from a state of order to a state of disorder. Things are breaking down, wearing out, deteriorating. In a cosmos governed by such a principle, one would expect that destruction, despair, and death would run rampant—perhaps to the exclusion of all else.

However, in the midst of this universe of entropy there exists the concept of good. People instinctively know the difference between right and wrong. Compassion exists. Love exists. And there is an innate human desire to bring order from chaos.

What caused the existence of good? Why do human beings crave order and harmony; not destruction, evil, and chaos?

The Bible's
Perfect Prophecies

The Bible indicates that prophecy is a test of something being from God, because only God can foretell the end from the beginning:

> *Remember the former things, those of long ago;*
> *I am God, and there is no other;*
> *I am God, and there is none like me.*
> *I make known the end from the beginning,*
> *from ancient times, what is still to come.*
> —ISAIAH 46:9-10

In Deuteronomy 18 and elsewhere in the Bible, we see how prophecy is involved in testing whether something is from God. Therefore, we might expect the Bible to contain prophecy—much of it, all perfectly correct—if the Bible really is inspired by God.

Estimates regarding the number of prophecies in the Bible vary greatly. In his personal quest to verify the existence of God (told in the book *A Skeptic's Search for God*), the author sorted out all of what he considered "provable" historical prophecies in the Bible.[44] Prophecies that could not be verified by archaeology, history, or by a fulfillment recorded by an author different from the author of the prophecy were not included. This resulted in a list of 118 historically verifiable nonmessianic prophecies, and 76 messianic ones (194 in total)—all of which came true.

This list of prophecies includes many of incredible precision. Some examples are:

❖ Predicting in detail the first exile of the Jews to Babylon (see reason 89), including the exact number of years the exile would last. Even the precise name of the leader who would allow the Jews to return to Israel was prophesied.

❖ Predicting 400 years of history (see reason 91).

❖ Predicting the second return of the Jews to Israel (see reason 8).

❖ Predicting the day Jesus would enter Jerusalem as king (see reason 67).

❖ Predicting the ancestors of Jesus (see reason 93).

As these few examples demonstrate, the prophecies are both precise and also highly unlikely to occur randomly. The odds of the coincidental occurrence of any of the above examples would be very remote—on the order of 1 chance in many thousands or millions.

However, for argument's sake, what would be the odds of all of the 194 prophecies—taken together—coming true if a probability of just 1 chance in 10 were applied to each? (This is extremely conservative since the actual odds would be far more remote.) Mathematically, the odds of 194 prophecies all coming true—with none being false—would be 1 chance in 10 multiplied 194 times. Scientists express it as 1 chance in 10^{194}—or one chance in ten with 194 zeros after it. These odds are virtually zero.

It is helpful to relate this small number to something more understandable. For example, one reason why playing state lotteries is not recommended is, among other things, the very remote odds of winning—about 1 chance in 10 million. While winning one lottery is extremely difficult (it's far more likely that one would be struck by lightning during one's lifetime), winning two lotteries in a row is virtually unheard of—it would probably shut down a state lottery for fraud investigation. The probability of 194 prophecies coming true with none wrong—with a 1 chance in 10 probability for each—would be like winning a total of about 28 lotteries in a row with a purchase of one ticket per lottery!

Another way of looking at the small odds is to break down all the matter in the universe into subatomic particles—protons, electrons, neutrons, quarks, and so on. That means all 100 billion stars and planets in each of the 100 billion galaxies are all broken down into subatomic particles. The result is about 10^{82} particles. Imagine marking one of these tiny subatomic particles. Now imagine asking a blindfolded person to randomly select one of the 10^{82}. There would be far greater odds of correctly picking the marked particle out of the entire universe twice over than for all the provable prophecies in the Bible to randomly come true.

The conclusions that come from evaluating the prophecies of the Bible touch on all three critical areas of belief we've seen in this book:

1. *God exists.* Otherwise such perfect prophecy would not be possible.

2. *The Bible is inspired by God.* Otherwise it would not contain such perfectly fulfilled prophecy.

3. *Jesus is the Son of God,* as He claimed, because He correctly prophesied His own death and resurrection, and because so many messianic prophecies were accurately fulfilled by Him.

Afterword:

How to "Move Mountains"

Perhaps your *101 Reasons* journey of faith has led you to a first-time reason to consider God, Jesus, or the Bible. Perhaps it has given you motivation to finally accept the Jesus of the Bible as Lord and Savior. Or perhaps it has motivated you to boldly proclaim the Bible's message. Whatever the case, your strengthened faith can help you "move mountains." (Matthew 17:14-20).

Skeptics Can "Move Mountains"

What could be more significant than finally discovering God? If a discovery of God leads to having a relationship with an infinite Creator for eternity, it would be far more significant than moving any literal mountain here on Earth.

As the 101 reasons show, there is substantial evidence of God's existence, of the reality of Jesus as God's Son, and of the reliability of the Bible as God's inspired Word. Evidence is often simple— observable in the creation that is around us. Evidence is also logical and based on thoughtful consideration of philosophical arguments. Evidence is available through archaeology and history. Evidence is available through science. And evidence is available through statistical analysis of things like the impossibility of evolution and the proof of the inspiration of the Bible through prophecy.

However, mere knowledge of this evidence is useless unless action is taken. Since the evidence points to the reliability of the Bible, it only makes sense that the Bible should be the authority to use in determining what a skeptic should do to have an eternal relationship with God. The Bible says,

> God so loved the world that he gave his one and only Son, that whoever believes in him shall not perish but have eternal life. For God did not send his Son into the world to condemn the world, but to save the world through him. Whoever believes in him is not condemned, but whoever does not believe stands condemned already because he has not believed in the name of God's one and only Son.
>
> —John 3:16-18

> Jesus answered, "I am the way and the truth and the life. No one comes to the Father except through me. If you really knew me, you would know my Father as well. From now on, you do know him and have seen him."
>
> —John 14:6-7

These verses and others clarify that the means of establishing a relationship with the God of the universe is by believing in— which also means accepting—God's Son, Jesus.

How to Have a Relationship with God

Anyone can have a personal relationship with God by following these steps and praying a simple, sincere prayer:

1. Believe that God exists and that He came to earth in the human form of Jesus Christ (see John 3:16; Romans 10:9).

2. Accept God's free forgiveness of sins and gift of new life through the death and resurrection of Jesus Christ (see Ephesians 1:7-8; 2:8-10).

3. Switch to God's plan for your life (see 1 Peter 1:21-23; Ephesians 2:1-7).

4. Expressly make Jesus Christ the Director of your life (see Matthew 7:21-27; 1 John 4:15).

Prayer for Eternal Life with God

"Dear God, I believe You sent Your Son, Jesus, to die for my sins so I can be forgiven. I'm sorry for my sins, and I want to live the rest of my life the way You want me to. Please put Your Spirit in my life to direct me. Amen."

Next Steps

People who sincerely take the above steps become members of God's family of believers. A new world of freedom and strength is available through prayer and obedience to God's will. New believers can also build their relationship with God by taking the following steps:

❖ Find a Bible-based church you like and attend regularly.

❖ Try to set aside some time each day to pray and read the Bible.

❖ Locate other Christians to spend time with on a regular basis.

New Believers in Jesus Can
"Move Mountains"

A relationship with the God of the universe opens new doors to great joy:

> *The kingdom of heaven is like treasure hidden in a field.*
> *When a man found it, he hid it again, and then in his*
> *joy went and sold all he had and bought that field.*
> —MATTHEW 13:44

> *Again, the kingdom of heaven is like a merchant*
> *looking for fine pearls. When he found one of great*
> *value, he went away and sold everything he had and*
> *bought it.*
> —MATTHEW 13:45-46

This joy has many aspects. First, there is the peace that comes from turning one's life over to Jesus, recognizing that God is in control. Second, there is joy in knowing that one can turn to God for answers and help in any situation, and that He is always there and hears all prayers. And third, there is the joy that comes from knowing that one's eternity is secure—that one will spend forever with God in paradise.

But in order to tap into the joy that God offers—joy that increases along with faith—one must grow in relationship with Him. In other words, there must be ongoing communication with Him, and receptiveness to His guidance. Having a daily quiet time in which to pray and to read the Bible is recommended. This time is a good time to sense God's presence and to "listen" for His answers. It's amazing how often the Bible verses one reads in a morning quiet time can apply to a situation one is facing.

Other ways in which one's communication, understanding of God, and faith can develop are

❖ finding a church and attending it regularly

❖ joining in fellowship activities with other believers in Christ

❖ listening to biblically based teaching on quality Christian TV and radio stations

❖ reading good Christian books

The more one's experience of communicating with God grows, the more answered prayers are revealed. As a result, faith grows even greater, and communication with God further increases. It is a rich, rewarding cycle.

Emboldened Christians Can "Move Mountains"

Some who read this book already have faith in God, Jesus, and the Bible. This text has merely strengthened it. How can such strengthened faith "move mountains"?

As the disciples grew in faith by encountering the risen Christ, they changed in character. They became bold—unafraid to tell others the good news of the resurrection of Jesus Christ. Likewise, *101 Reasons You Can Believe* provides 101 ways to talk to a nonbeliever about Jesus.

Sometimes people are afraid to talk to others about Jesus. But it's really not as difficult as is thought. And the information in this book can help. Here is one effective approach to using the evidence in this book to talk to a nonbeliever:

1. Establish a friendly relationship with an individual.

2. Discuss various topics and discover what interests him or her.

3. Focusing on the person's area of interest (that is, science, history, philosophy, nature, and so on), bring one of the 101 reasons to the individual's attention in a nonthreatening way to pique his or her interest.

4. Discuss the reason, leading to the conclusion about God, Jesus, or the Bible.

5. In future discussions, additional reasons can be gone over, with the eventual goal of introducing the gospel to the person.

6. Invite the individual to church or to some social gathering with fellow Christians.

7. Present the gospel to the individual, explaining how he or she may have a relationship with God.

What mountain could be more significant than helping another peson gain an eternal relationship with God?

Continue to Seek God

Certainly there are far more than 101 reasons you can believe. As the author of the book of Hebrews points out, God "rewards those who earnestly seek him" (11:6).

While experiencing the world around us, we should start to look for "reasons to believe." They are everywhere—in nature, in accomplishments, in ideas. Once we develop the mindset that the God of creation is behind virtually everything, the miraculous nature of things becomes more apparent.

Naysayers and skeptics may scoff at the evidence of God. Yet they simply can't provide explanations for the evidence all around us.

❖ Perhaps they say a rose "evolved"—but they don't know how.

❖ Perhaps they believe someone stole Jesus' body—but they don't know why Roman and Jewish search teams couldn't locate it.

❖ Perhaps they think Beethoven was a genius—but they can't explain why.

❖ Perhaps they enjoy the taste of an orange—but they don't know why it tastes so good.

❖ Perhaps they think the outcome of biblical prophecies is "luck"—but they would never think that engineering design, which uses the same statistical methods, is "luck."

❖ Perhaps they think the human eye just "happened"—but can't imagine how all its parts came about at the same time so it could actually function.

God has provided us with a mind to think—so we can rationally, logically examine the evidence of the world around us. If we do so in an objective manner, there are three conclusions we can ultimately draw:

That God is real.
That Jesus is who He claimed to be—God in human form.
That the Bible is inspired by God—and is reliable.

Questions
for Building Faith

	7. Accepting God in Strength
	6. Knowing God in Soul
	5. Appreciating God in Mind
	4. Feeling God in Heart
	3. Verifying God in History
	2. Pursuing God in Science
	1. Observing God in Nature

Building faith is a process, one that involves 1) seeking God, 2) building belief, and 3) eventually developing strong, reasoned faith (see pages 9–10).

101 Reasons You Can Believe can help people from all backgrounds develop faith through the consideration of a variety of things: nature, science, history, philosophy, and emotional and logical exploration of God. The illustration above shows a process for the building of faith that can "move mountains," such as the one using the questions on the following pages.

Individuals can use these questions as a method to build faith by exploring God on a daily basis. For example, during daily devotions a small amount of time can be set aside to ponder one of the questions using the text and the Bible. The material in *101 Reasons You Can Believe* can be completed in five weeks.

Likewise, groups can briefly consider one of the seven following topics each week for a seven-week exploration. Or, if preferred, an in-depth study could extend to 35 weeks, on a one-question-per-week basis.

The questions build on one another by: 1) exploring what is observable about God, 2) exploring what is quantifiable and verifiable, 3) reviewing philosophical areas, and finally 4) coming face-to-face with God's Son.

1. Observing God in Nature

Since the creation of the world God's invisible qualities—his eternal power and divine nature—have been clearly seen, being understood from what has been made, so that men are without excuse.

—ROMANS 1:20

What could be more revealing about the Creator than the creation? From the heavens, to the mountains, to the creatures, to individual cells of life, God's existence is clearly seen. *Reasons 9, 15, 20, 39, 41, 45, 47, 54, 60, 64, 66, 71, 76, 84, 95, 99.*

1. The Psalmist said, "The heavens declare the glory of God" (Psalm 19:1). Discuss various ways in which this glory is visible to us (71).

2. God has provided many things on earth for our benefit. Discuss some that are apparent (41, 84, 99). Discuss some that are not apparent (15, 54, 64).

3. The creatures of the earth reveal God in many ways: first, in their amazing capabilities (9, 47); second, in their incredible ability to survive (60, 95); and third, in their surprising instincts (76). How does this diversity add to a more complete understanding of God?

4. The monarch butterfly provides a fascinating model of a metamorphosis from one state of life to another (20). What can this teach us about the stages of life and death?

5. The more we understand about our human bodies, the more we "see" God (39, 45, 66). What are some of the things you have learned that are most surprising and that have revealed God most vividly to you?

2. Pursuing God in Science

He rewards those who earnestly seek him.
—HEBREWS 11:6

The more science adds to our knowledge, the more we realize that the words of the Bible have been accurate all along. Now, exciting new discoveries reveal the unmistakable hand of the Creator. *Reasons 2, 5, 12, 32, 36, 37, 43, 49, 51, 53, 62, 69, 74, 79, 88, 92.*

1. Discuss recent discoveries that disprove the theory of evolution in favor of creation by a loving God as outlined in Genesis (2, 12, 53).

2. Recent discoveries about the big bang and general relativity confirm that time had a beginning. In what way do these discoveries add significantly to biblical claims (43, 49)?

3. Incredible discoveries about the universe indicate that God is a Designer beyond time and space. How do black holes, gravity, and the "amazing timed collision" indicate a multidimensional God (37, 51, 74)?

4. Evidence clearly shows that planet Earth was carefully planned for man by God. What things indicate this? Is it important whether or not He may have designed another such planet in the universe (36, 69, 88)?

5. God's design extends into even the innermost workings of our bodies. How do such things as the complexity of sight (79), red blood cells (92), ATP motors (5), the regeneration of our body (32), and the amazing xi particle (62) point to a Designer God?

3. Verifying God in History

Remember the wonders he has done, his miracles,
and the judgments he pronounced.
　　　　　　　　　　　　　—1 Chronicles 16:12

Christianity has the distinction of being historically based. Therefore, if the Bible is to be used as the ultimate authority, we must be able to know it is consistent with history. In fact history, archaeology, and prophecy point to biblical accuracy and to an omnipotent God. *Reasons 8, 10, 16, 21, 28, 35, 38, 42, 48, 52, 57, 61, 65, 70, 78, 82, 85, 89, 91, 96.*

1. Read Isaiah 46:9-10. There are many significant prophecies regarding the Jews that reveal the presence of God. Discuss those that are most interesting or compelling to you (8, 89, 91, 96).

2. What do the discoveries of biblical archaeological sites tell us (10, 16, 28, 48, 57, 70, 82, 85)?

3. Archaeological discoveries often reveal information about people or customs of the time. How do such discoveries help build faith in the God of the Bible (21, 35)?

4. If we are to regard the miraculous prophecies in the Bible as genuine, it is imperative that we can be able to trust the

biblical manuscripts. Discuss how archaeological discoveries help us do this (42, 52, 61, 65).

5. As with a hostile witness, when a great archaeologist sets out to disprove the Bible and ends up converting to Christianity it adds great credibility. Discuss (38, 78).

4. Feeling God in Heart

Love the Lord your God with all your heart.
—MARK 12:30

Embedded within every human being are feelings and emotions that can't be measured by any of our senses. Nor can they be measured by any scientific instrument (only subsequent responses can be measured). Yet we know these things are real. *Reasons 1, 18, 23, 24, 29, 44, 50, 68, 81, 97, 100.*

1. Why was it necessary for God to create human beings with emotions (18, 44)?

2. God didn't have to create a world with pleasurable experiences, yet He did. Why do you think God provided pleasure (1, 29, 97)?

3. Emotional instincts that give rise to care for others and to joy have been placed in human beings. How does this reveal the hand of God (24, 50)?

4. Special gifts that inspire vast numbers of people have been given to certain individuals. Why would God have provided the world with such gifted people (23, 68)?

5. Hope is a very special trait within the human race. Discuss how God provides hope, and why (81, 100).

5. Appreciating God in Mind

Love the Lord your God with all your...mind.
—Mark 12:30

An important part of loving God is acknowledging His existence and majesty using the mind He has provided us. While some choose to "reason" the nonexistence of God, in reality, the more carefully and objectively we intellectually consider God, the more real and multidimensional He becomes. *Reasons 4, 7, 13, 17, 19, 22, 30, 40, 56, 63, 94.*

1. Discuss information processing—from an individual DNA molecule of a fertilized egg, through the development of all the specialized stages of a fetus, to a fully developed baby. How does the system know what to do? When? Where? And to what extent? How does this reveal God (17)?

2. Human beings have capacities such as thought and logic that can't be understood by any naturalistic system. How do these phenomena relate to God (4, 40, 56, 94)?

3. How can laws of physics contradict each other? And how do such laws—combined with existence in and of itself—fit into the reality of a multidimensional God (7, 22, 30)?

4. Why do you suppose God provided humans with the foresight to protect themselves from disease (13, 19)?

5. How can atheism actually be used to support the reality of God (63)?

6. Knowing God in Soul

Love the Lord your God with all your...soul.
—MARK 12:30

There is an indefinable connection between human beings and the supernatural that we call spirit, or soul. To some people it's as real as any emotion, yet to others it seems fanciful. Philosophers call this view of body and soul *dualism,* and that concept is accepted by most of the world. Something must exist to explain the inherent beliefs and tendencies of human beings that are beyond the physiological realm. *Reasons 11, 25, 27, 32, 34, 55, 58, 72, 77, 83, 86, 90, 100.*

1. What evidence is there that a soul really exists? How does a soul provide evidence of God (32, 77)?

2. Discuss how intrinsic instincts such as the belief in God, the need to worship, the existence of good, or the existence of purpose reveal God and His desired relationship with human beings (11, 55, 90, 100).

3. How do paradoxes and unique natural phenomena such as infinity and light point to the existence of God (25, 27, 34)?

4. Human beings are afforded amazing abilities such as free will, the ability to imagine freely, and the ability to communicate ideas through speech. In what ways might this show a spiritual connection with God (72, 83, 86)?

5. God's communication to human beings often affects them through life-changing experiences. Think of people you

know (maybe yourself) who have been changed by God's love. Discuss (58).

7. Accepting God in Strength

Love the Lord your God with all your...strength.
—MARK 12:30

Thorough development of faith in God results in our loving Him with all our heart, soul, mind, and strength. Loving God with strength (actions) leads to recognizing Jesus as the Messiah—God incarnate—and then accepting him as Lord and Savior. Abundant evidence exists to allow us to be assured that Jesus is who He claimed to be: the divine Savior of the world. *Reasons 3, 6, 14, 26, 31, 33, 46, 59, 67, 73, 75, 80, 87, 93, 98, 101.*

1. Imagine you are a member of the Sanhedrin (the governing Jewish religious body) on the day of the resurrection. What steps would you suggest to locate Jesus' missing corpse? Why would finding it be so important (3, 6)?

2. Information about Jesus comes from eyewitnesses, from once-hostile witnesses who changed, and from authors who acknowledge His existence but didn't believe He rose from the dead. Discuss the importance of each of these groups of people in building faith (31, 75, 87).

3. Perhaps the most compelling evidence supporting the historicity of the resurrection is the martyrdom of the apostles and other early Christians. Why would this be so meaningful (26, 98)?

4. Refer to Isaiah 46:9-10. Since 100-percent perfect prophecy is something only God can do, discuss the prophecies of Jesus and how they demonstrate He is the Messiah (14, 59, 67, 73, 93, 101).

5. Why is it so important that Jesus Himself prophesied—and did so accurately (33, 80)?

Notes

1. Ralph Muncaster, *Dismantling Evolution: Building the Case for Intelligent Design* (Eugene, OR: Harvest House Publishers, 2003), p. 142.

2. Josh McDowell, *The Resurrection Factor* (San Bernardino, CA: Here's Life Publishers, Inc., 1989), pp. 56-57.

3. http://www.runningdeerslonghouse.com/webdoc238.htm.

4. http://www.peripatus.gen.nz/paleontology/CamExp.html.

5. Stephen J. Gould, "Is a New and General Theory of Evolution Emerging?" *Paleobiology,* vol. 6 (1980), p. 40; as cited on Genesis Park Web site (www.genesispark.org).

6. Eusebius, *Life of Constantine,* 3:41, as cited by John McRay, *Archaeology and the New Testament* (Grand Rapids, MI: Baker Book House, 1991), p. 156.

7. http://www.padfield.com/tours/cmphoto2.html.

8. http://hyperphysics.phy-astr.gsu.edu/hbase/optmod/qualig.html.

9. Stephen W. Hawking, *A Brief History of Time—From the Big Bang to Black Holes* (New York: Bantam Books, 1988), p. 125.

10. Dr. Norman Geisler, "The Till-Geisler Debate" (http://www.angelfire.com/co/jesusFreak/resources.html).

11. Richard A. Swenson, *More Than Meets the Eye: Fascinating Glimpses of God's Power and Design* (Colorado Springs, CO: NavPress, 2000), p. 24.

12. Fred Heeren, *Show Me God: What the Message from Space is Telling Us about God* (Wheeling, IL: Daystar Productions, 1998), p. 306.

13. Josh McDowell, *The New Evidence that Demands a Verdict* (Nashville, TN: Thomas Nelson Publishers, 1999), p. 38.

14. Norman L. Geisler and William E. Nix, *A General Introduction to the Bible,* (Chicago: Moody Press, 1980), p. 361.

15. Hugh Ross, "WMAP Offers Spectacular Proofs of Creation Event," *Connections,* Second Quarter 2003 (Pasadena, CA: Reasons to Believe), p. 6.

16. Michael J. Behe, *Darwin's Black Box: The Biochemical Challenge to Evolution* (New York: The Free Press, 1996), pp. 15-21; Richard A. Swenson, *More Than Meets the Eye: Fascinating Glimpses of God's Power and Design* (Colorado Springs, CO: NavPress, 2000), pp. 31-33.

17. Lee Dye, "Casts Reveal Ant Architecture," AntColony.org (http://www.ant-colony.org/news/plastermodels.htm).

18. F. F. Bruce, "Archaeological Confirmation of the New Testament," *Revelation and the Bible,* Carl Henry, ed. (Grand Rapids, MI: Baker Book House, 1969), pp. 327-328; as cited in McDowell, *The New Evidence,* p. 66.

19. http://www.thenazareneway.com/ossuary_of_james.htm.

20. http://www.livius.org/caa-can/caiaphas/.

21. Hugh Ross, *The Creator and the Cosmos,* 2nd ed. (Colorado Springs, CO: NavPress, 1995), p. 32.

22. Hugh Ross, "Speed of Gravity Measured, Scripture Validated," *Connections*, Second Quarter 2003 (Pasadena, CA: Reasons to Believe), p. 4.

23. McDowell, *The New Evidence,* p. 80.

24. Ross, *The Creator and the Cosmos,* 2nd ed., pp. 112-121.

25. Hugh Ross, "Metal Matters," http://www.reasons.org/resources/fff/2001 issue06/index.shtml?main#metal_matters.

26. Hugh Ross, *The Genesis Question* (Colorado Springs, CO: NavPress, 1998), pp. 51-52, 64-65, 150-154.

27. Swenson, p. 40.

28. Darold A. Treffert, *Extraordinary People: Understanding Savant Syndrome* (New York: Ballantine Books, 1989), p. 13, as cited in Swenson.

29. http://198.62.75.1/www1/ofm/san/BET03gos.html.

30. http://www.bible.ca/d-history-archeology-crucifixion-cross.htm.

31. http://www.enchantedlearning.com/subjects/invertebrates/jellyfish/Jelly-fishcoloring.shtml.

32. Samuel Davidson, *The Hebrew Text of the Old Testament* (London: 1856), p. 89; as cited in Norman L. Geisler and William E. Nix, *A General Introduction to the Bible.* (Chicago: Moody Press, 1986).

33. Swenson, p. 20.

34. http://www.nationalgeographic.com/features/96/lightning/3a.html.

35. Eugene Linden, "How the Earth Maintains Life," *Time*, November 13, 1989, p. 114, as cited by Fred Heeren, *Show Me God, What the Message*

from Space Is Telling Us About God, (Wheeling, IL: Searchlight Publications, 1995), p. 180.

36. http://www.israelmagictours.com/English/ascension_church.htm.

37. http://www.bible-history.com/quotes/william_f_albright_3.html.

38. Swenson, p. 34.

39. Hugh Ross, *The Creator and the Cosmos,* 3rd ed. (Colorado Springs, CO: NavPress, 2001), pp. 195-198.

40. Swenson, pp. 23-25.

41. http://www.census.gov/ipc/www/worldhis.html.

42. Brian Moynahan, *The Faith: A History of Christianity* (New York: Doubleday, 2002), p. 52.

43. Moynahan, p. 14.

44. Ralph O. Muncaster, *A Skeptic's Search for God* (Eugene, OR: Harvest House Publishers, 2002), pp. 141-157, 163-189.

Bibliography

Archaeology and the Bible: The Best of BAR, Vol. 1, "Early Israel." Washington, DC: Bible Archaeology Society, 1990.

Archaeology and the Bible: The Best of BAR, Vol. 2, "Archaeology in the World of Herod, Jesus and Paul." Washington, DC: Bible Archaeology Society, 1990.

The Complete Word Study of the Old Testament. Chattanooga, TN: AMG Publishers, 1991.

Crossan, John Dominic, and Jonathan L. Reed. *Excavating Jesus.* New York: HarperCollins Publishers, 2001.

Eerdman's Handbook to the Bible. Littlemore, Oxford, England: Lion Publishing, 1973.

Elwell, Walter A., ed. *Evangelical Dictionary of Theology.* Grand Rapids, MI: Baker Book House, 1984.

Finegan, Jack. *The Archeology of the New Testament.* Princeton, NJ: Princeton University Press, 1992.

Foxe, John. *The New Foxe's Book of Martyrs.* North Brunswick, NJ: Bridge–Logos Publishers, 1997.

Free, Joseph P., and Howard F. Vos, *Archaeology and Bible History.* Grand Rapids, MI: Zondervan, 1969.

Gardner, Joseph L., ed. *Reader's Digest Who's Who in the Bible.* Pleasantville, NY: Reader's Digest Association, Inc., 1994.

Geisler, Norman and Ron Brooks. *When Skeptics Ask: A Handbook of Christian Evidences.* Grand Rapids, MI: Baker Books, 1990.

Glynn, Patrick. *God: The Evidence.* Rocklin, CA: Forum, 1999.

Habermas, Gary. *The Historical Jesus.* Joplin, MO: College Press Publishing Company, Inc., 1996.

The Harper Atlas of the Bible. New York: Harper & Row, 1987.

Hoehner, Harold W. *Chronological Aspects of the Life of Christ*. Grand Rapids, MI: Zondervan Publishing House, 1977.

http://www.bible-history.com.

http://www.bible-researcher.com.

http://www.catacombsociety.org.

http://www.christianstudycenter.com.

http://www.facingthechallenge.org.

http://www.neverthirsty.org.

http://www.tektonics.org.

Josephus, Flavius, tr. William Whiston. *The Complete Works of Josephus*. Grand Rapids, MI: Kregel, 1981.

Keely, Robin. *Jesus 2000*. Batavia, IL: Lion Publishing, 1989.

Life Application Bible. Wheaton, IL: Tyndale House Publishers, 1991.

McBirnie, William Steuart. *The Search for the Twelve Apostles*. Wheaton, IL: Living Books, 1973.

McDowell, Josh, and Bill Wilson. *A Ready Defense*. San Bernardino, CA: Here's Life Publishers, Inc., 1990.

McDowell, Josh, and Bill Wilson. *The New Evidence that Demands a Verdict*. Nashville, TN: Thomas Nelson Publishers, 1990.

McDowell, Josh. *The Resurrection Factor*. San Bernadino, CA: Here's Life Publishers, Inc., 1989.

McRay, John. *Archaeology and the New Testament*. Grand Rapids, MI: Baker Book House, 1991.

Moreland, J.P., and Kai Nielsen. *Does God Exist? The Debate between Theists and Atheists*. Amherst, NY: Prometheus Books, 1993.

Moynahan, Brian. *The Faith*. New York: Doubleday, 2001.

Packer, J.I., Merrill C. Tenney, and William White Jr. *Illustrated Encyclopedia of Bible Facts*. Nashville, TN: Thomas Nelson, Inc., 1980.

Price, Randall. *The Stones Cry Out*. Eugene, OR: Harvest House, 1997.

Readers Digest ABC's of the Bible. Pleasantville, NY: 1994.

Ross, Hugh. *The Creator and the Cosmos: How the Greatest Scientific Discoveries of the Century Reveal God*, 3rd ed. Colorado Springs, CO: NavPress, 2001.

Schroeder, Gerald L. *The Science of God*. New York: Broadway Books, 1997.

Shanks, Hershel, ed. *Understanding the Dead Sea Scrolls*. New York: Vintage Books, 1993.

Smith, F. LaGard. *The Daily Bible in Chronological Order*. Eugene, OR: Harvest House, 1984.

Strobel, Lee. *The Case for Christ*. Grand Rapids, MI: Zondervan Publishing House, 1998.

Swenson, Richard A. *More than Meets the Eye: Fascinating Glimpses of God's Power and Design*. Colorado Springs, CO: NavPress, 2000.

Unger, Merrill F. *The New Unger's Bible Handbook*. Chicago: Moody Press, 1984.

Vos, Howard F. *Introduction to Church History*. Nashville, TN: Nelson, 1994.

Walvoord, John F. *The Prophecy Knowledge Handbook*. Wheaton, IL: Victor Books, 1990.

Youngblood, Ronald F. *New Illustrated Bible Dictionary*. Nashville, TN: Nelson, 1995.

The Ministry of Strong Basis to Believe and Ralph O. Muncaster

Is there evidence of God's existence?

Is the Bible really true?

A former atheist and hard-core skeptic, Ralph Muncaster spent 15 years conducting research, with the original intent of refuting the Bible. Armed with an engineering education and a critical, questioning mind, he was certain that the Bible could not possibly be consistent with such sciences as anthropology, molecular biology, and physics.

To his surprise, the more he searched, the more evidence he found—evidence that supports the Bible's claims. In 1986, Ralph became aware of the prophetic accuracy of the Bible. He recognized that such precision was "statistically impossible." Investigating the scientific and historical documentation and its consistency with the Bible, he was startled by his findings: Manuscripts written thousands of years ago contain information that could not possibly have been known at that time...without divine intervention.

Now, having taught Christian apologetics at the university level, Ralph is a frequent lecturer at colleges and churches and for other organizations on topics of apologetics, world religions, and biblical authority. He is the founder of Strong Basis to Believe, a ministry started in 1991 that has been expanded in scope to touch hundreds of churches and organizations. He has taught thousands of skeptics, church leaders, and pastors throughout the world. He holds a BS in engineering and an MBA from the University of Colorado.

Ralph continues to build on his Examine the Evidence® series of apologetic booklets (from Harvest House Publishers), a fascinating exploration of various issues of the Christian faith. Each book provides extensive information about a single topic and presents clearly stated, charted, and detailed evidence to skeptics, seekers, and Christians. In addition, his highly popular *Creation vs. Evolution* book is available as a state-of-the-art two-hour videotape.

Along with the Examine the Evidence series, there is an integrated teaching program that is available through the ministry's Web site, www.evidenceofgod.com.

For answers to your questions and great information on how to talk about Jesus with the skeptics and seekers in your life, visit the Strong Basis to Believe Web site at:

www.evidenceofgod.com

You may contact us at:
Ralph O. Muncaster
PMB-212
26861 Trabuco Rd., Suite E
Mission Viejo, CA 92691
Phone: 714-628-8767
E-mail: ralphmuncaster1@yahoo.com

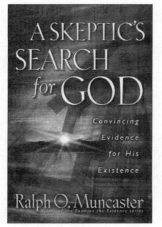

1,456 hours of Sunday school and church turned Ralph Muncaster into a hard-core atheist.

Then he was challenged to honestly investigate the Bible and the facts of modern science. He was stunned. Fact after fact—from biology, history, archaeology, physics—lined up with the Bible's account!

Join Ralph on the intensive personal search that took him—a cynical skeptic with an education in engineering—from disbelief to belief in God and the Jesus of the Bible. Along the way,

❖ you'll encounter the same astounding evidence that the author found during his three-year search

❖ you'll find solid information that challenges comfortable assumptions and outdated ideas

❖ your mind will be opened and your faith will be strengthened

Fascinating, unconventional, and provocative, *A Skeptic's Search for God* will point you to the facts—and to the God of the universe who is behind them.

"The dismantling of Darwinian evolution is long overdue…This book will be particularly helpful to the general reader looking for an easily accessible introduction to intelligent design."

—Dr. William Dembski, author of *Intelligent Design: The Bridge Between Science and Theology*

Enough Time + Enough Stuff = Life …Right?

In the few seconds it's taken you to read these words, trillions of molecular interactions have taken place in your eyes and brain. And this is just one of the amazing things that today's molecular biology has revealed about the complex inner workings of our cells.

The conclusion? We now know that even a 15-billion-year-old universe allows *far too little* time for life to arise through evolutionary random chance. As author Ralph Muncaster surveys some of the latest findings from biochemistry, astrophysics, and other fields, you'll discover further that

❖ the mechanisms of evolution—mutations and gradual change—fall apart in the face of the hard facts

❖ the random development of life is statistically impossible

❖ from the nucleus to the cosmos, everything we examine displays evidence of purposeful design

Exploring and revealing the magnificent complexity of the universe, *Dismantling Evolution* takes you beyond the data and gives you a glimpse of the Designer who's behind everything that exists.

**Tough Questions—Quick, Factual,
Convincing Answers**

The Examine the Evidence® Series
by Ralph O. Muncaster

Can Archaeology Prove the New Testament?

Can Archaeology Prove the Old Testament?

Can We Know for Certain We Are Going to Heaven?

Can You Trust the Bible?

Creation vs. Evolution:
What Do the Latest Scientific Discoveries Reveal?

Creation vs. Evolution VIDEO:
What Do the Latest Scientific Discoveries Reveal?

Dinosaurs and the Bible

Does the Bible Predict the Future?

How Do We Know Jesus Was God?

How Is Jesus Different from Other Religious Leaders?

How to Talk About Jesus with the Skeptics in Your Life

Is the Bible Really a Message from God?

Science—Was the Bible Ahead of Its Time?

What Is the Proof for the Resurrection?

What Is the Trinity?

What Really Happens When You Die?

Why Are Scientists Turning to God?

Why Does God Allow Suffering?